THE SHAMELESS FULL MOON, TRAVELS IN AFRICA

By Carol Miller

ABOUT THE AUTHOR:

I was a writer. All my life I had been a writer, and from age fifteen a paid journalist and then, after I went to Mexico in the early fifties, and stayed on, and on, I became a part of Mexico, a sculptress with a dazzling career, and also an interpreter, a translator, a traveler, an explorer in the pursuit of lost cultures. I stalked their ruins like a detective, delving into research, proposing new theories. I made a profession of explaining things, and describing things. And I made things, too, I *did* things: ceramic and interior design and table settings and even cooking, and I painted a bit. But then, I also had an iguana and a parrot and I bred Xoloitzcuintle dogs, that hairless wonder, harbinger of Xolotl, who crossed the river of death into the nine kingdoms of the Netherworld, and I bred puppies to save this remarkable species from extinction. I did all that, and more. I rode horses, and edited magazines and wrote, and wrote, and wrote: poetry, history, travel.

"Love. Fall in love and stay in love. Write only what you love, and love what you write. You have to get up in the morning and write something you love, something to live for." Ray Bradbury

Thank you, Tomás

PRELUDE

Mexico City, 2014, at my desk on a rainy Sunday morning, wrapped in a comforting lap rug of Chinese bamboo fibers and looking out over the nasturtiums pelted by yesterday's hailstones. "Do you miss Africa terribly?" I wrote to John, our friend from Perth, Australia, who had shared a few of our Zimbabwe days, most notably the shipwreck. A shipwreck in Zimbabwe, a landlocked country? Ah, but Lake Kariba...

"Does a part of your soul still yearn for the scent of the dew-damp grass and the hoarse grunting of the lion before dawn? Do you still hear the shriek of the fish-eagle? Does an elephant cross the path of your dreams in the murkiness before the sun emerges, with the glow of Africa streaking its colors?"

Sometimes I wonder how I can possibly go on and perhaps for that reason I wrote this book. I yearn for Africa as I might a close friend or a beloved relative. The longing is almost painful, touched with tenderness, surely a fact, a kind of mourning. There were other places—Greece and Egypt, Spain and Morocco, the Mediterranean world, the Adriatic world, Southeast Asia, China and India, Mongolia and Central Asia, Russia, Turkey, Iran, Syria, the Middle East, South America but especially Peru. There were Rapa Nui and French Polynesia, my own beloved Mexico, Europe of course, the U.S. obviously, all in the pursuit of the convergence of man's cultures, but also in the quest for the pieces of myself. And not only the tracing of cultures and their overlapping or mingling or enveloping and entwining; what about simple beauty? The staggering loveliness and sheer wonderment, not so simple at all. Has any of it remained? These cradles of civilizations toppled with the trees of their forests, the minerals in their ground, greed and growth, the expansion of some, the plowing under of others. Wars, investments, arms traders, stock brokers, diamond dealers. Does the world spin on as it always has or is something tangled?

I have no patience for the people who discount the Africans as "barely able to beat a drum", or who decry the continent as backward because it is not European. Or as degraded because it finds no reward in European values, European goals or European standards. It was Europe that created the notions of "backwardness" or "development", of "corruption" or "the rule of law" and it is Europeans and their offspring who have generally provoked, augmented or supported whichever of these seemed convenient to its larger policy, or consistent with its values. In January of 1906, according to Mary S. Lovell's biography, Winston Churchill went to Manchester, in England, to tour the worst slums. "Fancy living in these streets," he remarked to a companion, "never seeing anything beautiful, never eating anything savoury and never saying anything clever!" This could never happen in Africa, nor in Mexico either, for that matter. There is always something to celebrate, something strange and delicious to eat, a geranium perhaps, blooming brilliantly, indifferently, in an old tin can.

It was also Churchill, then an official in the Colonial Office, who made a trip to Britain's new possessions in East Africa. He disembarked in Mombasa and rode the "Uganda Railroad" of the British East Africa Railroad Company, which we would in time see for ourselves, on a bench attached to the cowcatcher, perilous but picturesque. At one point he found himself looking across a grassland at a rhinocerous, and he marveled at these wonderful animals, roaming here since prehistory, and then he shot it! Why do men feel compelled to collect trophies? Are they so afraid of forgetting something they think they should remember? Some things are better imagined than remembered.

As Heraclitus said, "God, to a goat, takes the form of a goat." The Africans have never had a problem with this, or with a plurality of convictions. The important thing is to accept things for what they are. Comparisons are fine if they serve to support what is, and is therefore worthy of recognition. But they are ignominious as justifications for a hypothesis either preconceived or taken out of context. The notion of past and future is a problem. There is only today.

Somehow I feel that in Africa the world began and here perhaps it might end. This is Eden: breathless, intact, suspended between origin and eternity. Everything has, in the course of evolution, become the by-product of something else, but Africa, the part I saw, the way I saw it, was pure and whole and untouched, despite colonialism and economic dependence and corruption or misery, disease and death, or even tourism.

CONTENTS

THE JOURNEY

The trip began in Paris on a Friday the thirteenth, 1989, under a full and blatant moon. The milling madhouse of Charles de Gaulle Airport was made somehow more enticing and less exasperating by a bomb threat which had hysterical female guards in uniform trying to clear an area that in the best of circumstances had been badly designed and which was hopelessly inefficient. The guard who confronted us was herself so upset as to be incoherent, so it was hard to know what she wanted or why, until we finally realized she wanted us out of there and dispatched to anywhere else at all. We went through security into the departure area, dragged our hand-baggage carts upstairs to the café and settled in until the flight was to be called. I decided to go exploring. Had barely descended the stairs on my way to the duty free shopping area when I heard a loud, sharp noise, sudden silence, then applause and a lot of bustling. Assumed a bomb had gone off, or at least had been harmlessly detonated in a closed space, so returned in terror, chagrined and pouting, to the café, very much less the bold explorer.

Our flight was bound for Nairobi, then would continue to Reunion, aboard a Boeing 747, but somehow it seemed larger than any other 747 I had ever seen. It was entirely outfitted for economy class, including the upper cabin, therefore permitting a total of four hundred and seventy-seven passengers, even today still a remarkable figure. This turned the plane into an outsized sardine can, designed to fly as many people as humanly—or inhumanly—possible the greatest distance, eight hours on the first leg. Since the flight departs at night and arrives just after dawn at Nairobi's then shabby but still respectable airport, the damage was minimum, or was so designed to be. Cramped muscles, leg spasms, perhaps a stiff neck. It just takes making up our mind that this is the way it must be and there is nothing to be done about it.

SATURDAY, OCTOBER 14

Swollen feet and very tired. Still an empty sensation, like hunger, from the bomb at the airport, a kind of delayed reaction, but that's how I am. I have to process things, like an outmoded computer, which of course back then was not even available. It has a name, anxiety, but I was new to this field, to this tightening of the solar plexus where the chakras meet.

There was a slight delay in the baggage claim area, not only due to the enormous number of passengers but because our luggage had been consigned to the Reunion container, which had therefore to be unloaded and revised. Took advantage of the time to change a little money to Kenyan shillings, highly appreciated currency whose removal from the country was then strictly prohibited.

When we finally emerged from the building—still marveling at the exchange rate of roughly twenty to twenty-two shillings to the dollar as opposed to Mexico's then fluctuating and unpredictable, even dangerous, parity—we were met by our driver and van. Alan, a rotund and congenial man who had been educated, like so many of his contemporaries, in a mission school, appeared in company uniform and was as resourceful as he turned out to be accommodating and agreeable. He was black, as were all the Abercrombie and Kent employees at all levels to be encountered, in both Tanzania and Kenya. We learned later that in Zimbabwe, formerly Southern

Rhodesia, they would turn out to be Zimbabwean whites, still resident in the country, though of course they have since left. Blacks were not then held in high esteem in southern Africa and in fact were dismissed with a pejorative huff: "african." The lower case is implicit in the inference.

The landscape, as we traveled toward Kenya's capital city, was much like the photographs I had admired and fussed over since childhood, a flat and dry country with the delicate silhouette of the thorny acacias so prized by the wandering giraffes, that nibbled at the uppermost reaches.

The city is a parody of a Gold Rush town, on the plains of the Athi River at the foot of the Kikuyu Hills, *"a place of extraordinary successes and extraordinary failures,"* as Beryl Markham wrote in 1942 in **West With the Night.** *"Its shops sell whatever you need to buy...it is a counting house in the wilderness."*

She describes Nairobi as the gateway to a still new country— new to foreigners, at any rate— a town that had sprung from a collection of corrugated iron shacks serving the spindly Uganda Railway *"to a sprawling welter of British, Boers, Indians, Somalis, Abyssinians, natives from all over Africa and a dozen other places. Its Indian Bazaar covers several acres; its hotels, its government offices, its race-course, and its churches are imposing evidence that modern times and methods have at last caught up with East Africa."*

The boardwalks have turned to cement, despite the signs that hang overhead, perpendicular to the sidewalk, to heighten the sense of a comic frontier town in a Western movie. Women, with few exceptions, are lumpy and dull in appearance, unless they are Masai and in such case would normally avoid Nairobi. The women we saw were generally thick-featured and squat. Their blackness was not a color but a condition, partly genetic and partly climatic— a black with a sheen and ebony depths, a rich and velvety black, a polished black like a pit with no end, a night without stars, the tunnel into nothingness, illuminated only by eyes and teeth and the bright wit of a kindly and capable people, with an enchanting sense of humor but visible want and limited means, the inevitable baby or perhaps several, and the burgeoning pregnancy. The world's greatest ill: over-population.

The men, with few exceptions, were lean and long, with chiseled features, small head and exorbitantly extended limbs: legs nine miles in length at the very least. They are beautiful, with an obvious influence—again, unless Masai, the ultimate aesthetic—of the refined flaring of nostrils and the soaring cheekbones we had seen in southern India or in the Arabs of the north, who came long ago to trade in Africa. Deep-set eyes, penetrating gaze, yet soft and soulful. And in fact, both the Indians and the Arabs have dominated trade in Africa for centuries. They have more imagination and fewer scruples.

The city back then was small, grid pattern, contained within the area roughly limited by the railroad station at one end and the university at the other. Beyond the railroad station spreads the doleful stain of the worst shantytown slum I had ever seen, surely one of the most sprawling and populous in the world.

At the upper end of town, beyond the university and the Synagogue, were the gambling casino, the Museum, Snake Park and the Institute for African Studies. Much beyond, a drive of perhaps thirty minutes, lies a splendid residential area not unlike Cuernavaca in Mexico, at the same altitude, fifteen hundred meters, and equally palm-shaded and flower drenched. We would see more of this later, at the end of our trip, at the invitation of the Mexican Ambassador and his wife.

A few buildings rise to fourteen or fifteen stories or even perhaps twenty. These are dwarfed, however, by the Convention Center, a cylindrical tower under which sits Jomo Kenyatta in bronze, in memory of the country's father, who distinguished himself during the struggle for independence from Britain, twenty-five years earlier.

A Common or esplanade served as a setting for the City Center area and the principal public buildings, mostly British Colonial or neo-Classic, otherwise post-World War II modern. The Intercontinental Hotel acted as another focus, for shops and services, but it was the Hilton, closer to the more traditional quarter, where the most action was concentrated. Still, I preferred the blocks above Kenyatta Avenue, beginning with "African Heritage", a kind of craft market arrangement that included artisan wares, native jewelry, bar, restaurant, traditional clothing or its modern spin-off, typical music, and continuing northward to the markets (bazaars), one for crafts and folklore, mostly baskets, and the other public, that is, fruit, vegetables, grains and meat. There were also the art galleries, design shops, a number of churches, the mosques, the *safari* outfitters—though the word *safari* in the local Swahili simply refers to a "journey" or "trip", nothing more—and our hotel, the Nairobi Safari Club.

The more exclusive hotels and restaurants were classified as "clubs" and therefore resolved the problem of "refusing admittance" on the basis of private membership. Guests were not "residents" but "members" and as such had to register any guests of their own. If I wished to invite the Mexican Ambassador and his wife for tea I had to register them at the entrance. If I wished to bring in an acquaintance of any class, sector or color to join me for breakfast or an interview I would probably be told, despite attempts at registration, that facilities were unavailable, unless the person were white, visibly prosperous or already known to the management. And these were blacks limiting blacks, but on the basis of class more than color, as would equally occur in Mexico City, New York or London. In Nairobi, however, the system was institutionalized and was never questioned, certainly not on the basis of "democracy" or the "politically correct and acceptable".

Nairobi in those days was graced by a number of galleries but while Black Africa was attempting its own view of itself in water color, oil, stone or bronze, the best art, as such, as we in the West conceive it to be, was from Nigeria and not easy to come by. The bronzes of Benin are magnificent, with a completely harmonious proportion and superb resolution of form. There was also much, back then, of worthy art, mostly allusive wood carving representing ancestor or spirit figures, from West Africa, but here in East Africa, a continent away, the best artistic expressions were to be found in textiles, jewelry and more commercial wood carving, the latter usually of tribal or animal figures. Best buys were finally narrowed to African amber (copal), those opaque but glowing yellow lumps of resin, like honey in the hand, that in time crack as ivory would, and were used in necklaces, the best examples of which ran to the thousands of dollars. We also liked the agate, hematite or malachite beads combined with silver elements, usually coin-silver Coptic crosses from Ethiopia (formerly Abyssinia) or Somalia, designs that refer to their origins in Oman or South India and evolved from the early Christianity and conversions of the Apostles: St. Mark in Egypt and Abyssinia, St. Thomas in Kerala and Madras (now Chennai).

Everyone sold what he had to offer. In Nairobi most of the available goods would seem to emphasize the folklore of the various tribes, as well as the diversity and novelty of the animals. To my immediate gratification, however, in Nairobi at least, and in fact most of Kenya, a matter of pride, was the scarcity of waste baskets fashioned from elephant feet or ashtrays of gorilla hands, the fly swatters of giraffe or zebra tails, crudely carved ivory that would have been better off in Chinese hands if not the original owner, and the badly dried and cracked skins of the nearly-extinct spotted cats or the pitifully wanting taxidermized heads of one or another among the horned trophies, mostly gazelles or antelope, as well as rhinocerous, whose numbers, once hundreds of thousands, are today absent from their natural habitat, in part thanks to the Chinese superstition, utterly false, regarding the aphrodisiac effects of powdered rhino horn. Curiously, this notion is not a recent phenomenon. It dates from the early caravan trade that linked China with the Mediterranean, and in time supplied rare and heavily coveted goods to the insatiable markets of Imperial Rome, later absorbed by Byzantium. The Turks and Arabs, too, sought rhino horn, that matted mixture of cartilage and hardened hair, as sheaths for their daggers. It would seem counter-indicated for the African countries to justify the slaughter of the very animals that attract visitors to their reserves, but tourism, though now fashionable and multitudinous, increasingly ceases to be an issue. African development would appear to be moving backward, predicated on the introduction of ill-advised and non-profitable crops, or the fallout from disease and civil war. *"Our notion of management, after all, is not theirs,"* Beryl Markham reminds us. *"Competitors in conquest have overlooked the vital soul of Africa herself, from which emanates the true resistance to conquest. The soul is not dead, but silent, the wisdom not lacking, but of such simplicity as to be counted non-existent in the tinker's mind of modern civilization."*

SUNDAY, OCTOBER 15

We visit the National Museum. It is modest and small but sincere, greatly limited but definitely miraculous in terms of the mileage gleaned from the funds or skills available. The model in the garden of an elephant named Ahmed pays homage to the largest tusker ever recorded. His skeleton stands inside, in the Museum's main hall, which is devoted to the natural sciences. Another area covers a little history, both ethnographic and political, including the Mao-Mao uprising that pressured for Independence. A crafts section and shop round out the visit.

Good bookstore, with a selection mostly originated in foreigners or Kenyans of European extraction, and includes the very articulate childhood of Elspeth Huxley (her husband was a cousin of Aldous'),

The Flame Trees of Thika. She was a friend of another author represented here, the Swiss-born Joy Adamson, *née* Friederike Victoria Gessner, author of **Born Free**, the story of the orphaned lion cub she and her husband George Adamson, a British gamekeeper, unwisely adopted, then trained to be released into the wild, a remarkable and, she was told, nearly impossible feat, since lions normally avoid humans. Their scent is repugnant. But once tamed, lions become completely dependent on their humans for survival. Elsa, the lioness, not only survived, but came home to visit, bringing her litter of cubs for Joy's inspection, and thus, another book. Joy and Elsa went on to become screen idols, won Oscars in 1966, and the late composer-conductor John Barry won his first of five Oscars for the song and the film score.

Beryl Markham's childhood and adult experiences, most of them hair raising, are also included, her vivid stories recounting her adventurous life, which extends to training race horses as well as solo flying, as she enters the new world of aviation. She made history on September 4, 1936, when she completed, and survived, the first solo flight by a woman, East to West across the Atlantic.

And then there is Karen Christence von Blixen-Finecke, born Karen Christenze Dinesen, whom we came to love through our Danish friends in Mexico during the fifties. They introduced us to the **Gothic Tales** she wrote under her pen name, Isak Dinesen. These include *Babette's Feast.* She also, in a labor of love and despair, wrote **The African Farm** and **Letters from Africa,** which screenwriter Kurt Ludke used as background for the script of Sidney Pollack's *Out of Africa* (1985), in part the motivation for our trip.

"I used to have a farm in Africa", sighs Meryl Streep with her carefully coached Danish accent, to the background of John Barry's sweeping music, another Oscar for the composer, and we begin to weep even before the film begins. She is looking out over the Kenyan grasslands from the window of the train, the onetime Uganda Equatorial Railroad, some of whose cars were restored

and refurbished for use in the film. (The others still service the run from Nairobi to Mombasa, as we shall see.)

We also found picture books in the Museum bookshop, very expensive but well worth every shilling, covering subjects as varied as the building of the Uganda Railroad (see: *The Ghost and the Darkness,* directed by Stephen Hopkins, 1996, script by William Goldman, the story of the two lions that obstructed the construction of the railroad bridge over the Tsavo River), and the annual year-long migration of a million wildebeest (or *gnu*).

Mary S. Lovell's biography of Beryl Markham further details the airborne adventures of this cohort of "Blix", Karen's outrageous husband, when incipient aviation was used to locate the herds to be pursued by the new visitors to Kenya, the "white hunters" or trophy collectors, but not only that: there were also those flights for carrying out ivory or for wartime reconnaissance. Beryl describes one gripping flight from Nairobi to Benghazi, as copilot to the Baron, and makes it brutally memorable. Blix, who could aim a rifle at a charging buffalo with his right hand, and down it with a clean shot between the eyes, while he discussed the relative merits of gin or whiskey in the "sundowner" in his left hand, was rarely sober.

We were catching on to a few elementary terms:

Asanti (sana): thank you
Tafadali: please
Kwaheri: goodbye
Jambó: good morning, good afternoon or just "hello!"
Karibu: you are welcome
Tuende: let's go
Pili-pili: spicy

Most languages invert two letters. Which two depends on the people and the peculiarities of their pronunciation. Here the inversion occurs with the "r" and the "l", exactly as with Chinese. So you never know whether to ask for "pili-pili" or "piri-piri". "Hot peppers" will do.

The language we were beginning to pick up is called *ki-Swahili*, "the tongue of the Swahil people". It takes its name from the *Swahil*, or coastal people, whose language became a mixture of *bantú* and Arab, later enriched with the idiom of the various tribes, extending from the peoples of Lake Turkana (formerly Rudolph) in the north to the bewitching Masai.

Among the most numerous of the peoples in central Kenya are the Kikuyu, whom Karen Blixen tried so hard to protect. They suffer particularly under laws imposed by Europe and standards imported according to foreign custom. The wealth of the Kikuyu was always judged on the basis of their cattle and goats, needed to make up a dowry. Each wife, in addition, required a separate hut in the village compound for herself and her children. The community would normally be dominated by the husband, in effect, the patriarch of the clan. Over-population, however, makes this increasingly unwelcome. And since a man can only properly be buried on his own land, inheritance laws further complicate the system.

The Masai, of course, those "princes of Eden", still live in close harmony with their habitat and infringe very little on the natural order. Other tribes are less in tune with the world around them. The game reserves and conservation areas are assigned the task of protecting the animals, despite the encroachment of human settlements. But the imposition is inevitable, as human population increases faster than its animal counterpart.

The parks are also legally authorized to discourage poaching, to the extent of exterminating a poacher if he is caught. No point taxing the already burdened justice system, officials feel, or of taking up valuable space in a crowded prison or of using state funds "to keep such vermin alive". Still, the whole thing gets caught up in a web as complex as it is anachronistic, at least from our point of view. It is probably as coherent as any other system but seems involved and impossible to regulate, in the struggle to keep the animals alive and nature in balance without toppling the considerations for a people plagued by the restrictions and requirements of their attempts at "development".

$$\iiint$$

The quiet, charming community of "Karen", named for the Baroness von Blixen, lies sixteen kilometers from Nairobi, toward the foot of the Ngong ("knuckle") Hills, among churches, golf club, giraffe farm, schools and cottages, all very white Protestant middle class, which pay homage in one way or another to the determined but unassuming Danish woman who lived in the stone house that is now a national museum. The film *Out of Africa* was actually shot in another, larger stone house, very similar but more isolated, to establish the illusion of life earlier in the century. The real Blixen house has already been encroached upon by such evidence of modernity as prefabricated buildings, a tractor in the field, someone's water tank.

The house is preserved much as she would have left it. Many of her personal effects, sold off after the debacle of the fire in her coffee factory, have been recovered and assembled for visitors to see: the dining room where she sat over coffee with her guests, telling the stories she would later publish; the library with Denys Finch-Hatton's collection of books; her bathtub; the bedroom with her hat, boots and jacket by a chair, a leopard skin on the floor and her white mosquito netting over the bed on which her shawl is laid.

The dishes are Limoges but not the original. Photographs reveal the faces of the principal characters in the drama of her life. The Baron Broor Blixen was a rascal, delightful or not, depending on the biographer, a man women found irresistible, a dashing friend and a daring hunter. Most researchers agree he was the model for Hemingway's Francis Macomber, he of the "short, happy life", and rumor takes it that many men, clients as well as close friends, would avoid at all cost introducing him to their wives. He was a heavy drinker who ended his life an alcoholic and he was pathologically generous, to the point of bankruptcy when the time came.

Denys, on the other hand, was tender, sensitive, erudite and much more subtly attractive. He was the picture of the withdrawn intellectual, though the movie made him into a taciturn anti-hero. He was apparently incapable of giving up his Masai companion or his male friendships, until they were taken from him. He was equally reluctant to renounce the open spaces of Samburu, Tsavo or the Masai Mara, and never committed to a relationship, with Karen or anyone. An unpublished letter perhaps describes him: *"He was afraid of being consumed by the fire of love, he was equally afraid of the fire in time going out, and leaving him cold."*

Denys was buried after the plane crash in the Ngong Hills, those voluptuous contours like clenched fists on the horizon outside Karen's window and beyond her green garden. In the film, however, the scene was shot in the Masai Mara, from a ridge overlooking the range. Below runs the river where Robert Redford washes Meryl Streep's hair. It stuck in my mind because a friend in Mexico made such a point of the scene's sensuality and, for her, unique communication. It had seemed like the most erotic of encounters, a poetic prelude to passion in the wild, and probably it was.

MONDAY, OCTOBER 16

We started in our little white van across the plain that skirts Nairobi National Park, bound for Namanga and the Tanzanian border. This was our first glimpse, and sound, of whistling acacia. These thorny bushes, virtually devoid of leaves, are dotted with round pods roughly the size of a quail's egg. The pods are pierced by ants and the holes become whistles when the wind blows through them.

We saw our first termite mounds, those miraculous earthen chimney stacks, so typical of Africa, that shield the most amazing and most tightly structured society in all the animal kingdom. And this led to random thoughts, as the sun rose in a whip-blue sky, of nationality as opposed to citizenship, or patriotism as related to a clan. It must take at least four generations to transform a society, since roots are such a personal matter, whether for termites or for men. The Federal Government, in effect, is no more than an expanded clan but much more impersonal and harder to comprehend, with its component roles less clearly defined.

This is Masai country, bony and hard. If it served any practical purpose it would surely have been expropriated but as it is, the tall nomadic figures in their red togas, carrying the long spears and rawhide shields, wander as they wish with their cattle, stalking the landscape and plucking at whatever pasture they might find, crossing and re-crossing the border at will and divulging the secrets of their perfect—though fly-specked—existence to no man, since no man would understand.

The farther we got from Nairobi and the few small towns near the road the more we encountered the increasingly numerous bands of Grant's gazelle, zebra and our first ostrich, a stately, solitary male, like a charcoal smudge in the thorny brush. Each time something moved I caught my breath. The sense of disbelief is highlighted with wonderment, the sensation—at first furtive and unspoken and then as time goes on, jubilant and ecstatic—of having discovered something unique, of seeing it all for the first time, of taking possession of the one thing that no human has ever before witnessed. Mankind, according to all indications, originated in Africa, but that was a long time ago. In the meantime, humans have lived with, or perhaps against, animals; and in our own time "wild animal parks" flourish, but for a westernized city dweller, despite

a lifetime of dogs and cats and horses among other random specimens, the notion of the primeval borders on pure magic.

The giraffe are especially unreal, surreal, distorted. The dream
becomes hallucination, the critical eye bewilderment. Their long
eyelashes glitter in the sun—as in an animated film—and their
curious gaze under the neat little horns, the lanky grace, the dis-
jointed movements, are like twelve-year-old boys: parts that move
but are not quite put together in the same rhythm. As time in Africa
wears on they become commonplace, though never for that reason
less remarkable. Yet the first glimpse, the long look through the
binoculars, the realization that this is a fact and can be breathed
on the wind, that it is not a film or a picture book or a nature documentary, like the sensation of the rubbery tongue on the awed hand
that feeds them at the giraffe farm in Karen, can never be really
assimilated.

We pass a number of Masai herdsmen. The men's hair is braided
into tiny plaits that fall like a curtain down their necks, washed
with cow's urine and stained with the rust-red earth. They love red,
anything red, everything red: the color of blood, of the earth, of the
sun beating down from a pitiless sky.

The women's heads are shaved, which brings out of the fine-
ness of their features, the firm set of their eyes, chiseled cheeks,
flashing eyes, "God's chosen ones". Writes Beryl Markham: *"What
upstart race, sprung from some recent, callow century to arm itself
with steel and boastfulness, can match in purity the blood of a single
Masai Murani, whose heritage may have stemmed not far from Eden?"*

Their plaid or checkered red robes and togas are now factory-
made cloth, and some of them even live in slat houses with laminated
metal roofs. They drink, while the vast plains move increasingly
beyond their reach. They yearn for the cattle they will never again
take into the bush and instead of challenging the lion they fear its
attack. When the Masai are wild and live in their circular settlements the lions give them a wide berth. Many say, and perhaps they

are right, that it might be the scent. The Masai are, indeed, a gamey lot, but their beauty, the elongated grace, the insolent dignity, serve them well. Most city people, especially government officials, steer clear of them; and most of them remain on the land, as they always have. Things are changing in East Africa but the Masai manage to hold back time.

1.

MASAI CHIEFTAIN

Their greatest problem is the anomaly of their wealth. To a Masai, prosperity is measured in cattle, the more the better. When necessary, a Masai could always barter a few head for the things he needed: his cloth, a bucket or two, a little salt, flour or sugar, to complement his standard diet of milk and blood. But Masai cattle are now a drug on the market and survival becomes increasingly precarious. On the other hand, the Masai keeps his numbers at a reasonable level. Like the animals around him: more pasture, more grazers, better hunting. Less grass, fewer animals, poor hunting. And so it is with the Masai. Like the lion, lean times, fewer cubs.

We reach the border. Namanga is much like a market town. Milling vendors, mostly Masai women proffering their beaded neck-pieces or crudely carved wooden necklaces, amulets, the opportunity, perhaps, to take their picture, while they bob—enticingly and a little obscenely—up and down. Once they thought the camera robbed them of their shadow but they have seen so many snapshots and the shadow remains, so why not charge? It seems perfectly reasonable. The only problem is that we left all our Kenya currency in an envelope with Anne, our A&K coordinator, back in Nairobi. Until

1

we cross the border and visit the bank on the Tanzania side, for the required exchange of fifty U.S. dollars per person, we will have nothing to spend. Foreign currency is strictly prohibited. There is too much contraband, in machine parts, foodstuffs, manufactured goods, anything one side has that the other has not.

The two countries, our guide remonstrates, "are insanely jealous of each other and officialdom maintains the animosity, precisely in order to discourage trade and fraternization. The Masai, of course, cross the frontier at will, as everyone is afraid of them, but they are the only ones."

The rest of us fill out the forms for our visas, then stand in line at the wooden hut, complete proceedings, and walk to the next shed: immigration, customs; then we say goodbye to Alan, who escorts us into the no-man's land where the vehicles are parked and transfers our things to the van of Eliud Veneti, who will now be our guide and driver. Alan will return to Nairobi with new passengers coming in from Tanzania, and Eliud will drive us out to the immigration officials on the other side.

Since Tanzania is not represented in Mexico's diplomatic community and visas have not been processed, as Kenya's were, by the British Embassy—Kenya is still a Commonwealth country—so we have to present our visa applications, photographs, fees and apologies, and then we are processed. It is all quite routine. The officials in turn apologize for charging more for a Mexican than for a U.S. citizen, turning first to Tomás and then to me. "It cannot be helped," they say, bowing slightly, in feigned humility and deference. Burocracy is more or less the same everywhere.

We proceed to the bank. Each facet of the operation is handled from a different queue or line. First we fill out the application, then pass to another line for it to be processed, then another line to watch the papers accumulate on the bank manager's desk.

We notice, with some dismay, that the applications, with their respective passports, are being piled on top of each other, as they appear, the earlier applications on the bottom, the more recent on the top. Before we have time to get overly agitated, however, the bank manager, grandly and ceremoniously, appears on the scene, sits down at his desk, draws the stack of applications toward him and turns them over with a thump. Now they are in order.

After the proper authorization we pass to another queue for the teller's window. The cashier counts out the bills while his assistant, jammed into the same cubicle at his side, sorts the bills into piles and then sheaths the piles, not with a paper clip or strip of paper but with one of the bank notes turned perpendicular to the others and folded over. This was done everywhere in Africa where we happened to change money.

♫♫♫

We are fairly close to the twin peaks of Kilimanjaro (Uhuru and Kibo) and can see their great bulk in the distance, riding the African rift, the north-south fault that traverses the entire continent. At 5,895 meters (19,341 feet) this is the tallest of Africa's mountains, in fact the highest free-standing mountain on earth, above sea level, pierced by Kibo, Mawenzi and Shira, its three volcanic vents or cones. The entire mountain complex is in fact itself a dormant volcano, held captive in Kilimanjaro National Park, very close to the border and to Amboseli Park, our destination in a week or ten days.

For the moment we are close to another rift landmark, the Longido Mountain, looming close to us, and to Mount Meru, at 4,565 meters (14,977 feet) a very respectable active stratovolcano, named for the Hindu navel of the earth, just seventy kilometers (forty-three miles) west of Kilimanjaro near the town of Arusha. This only active volcano around is called by the Masai "The Mountain of God". I remember in *Out of Africa* when Farah, Karen's servant, runs to wake the Baroness as the coffee factory goes up in flames and he tells her solemnly, "I think that God is coming." Now it makes sense.

Pillars of fire, whether witnessed by the Hindu, the Pre-Columbian cultures of Mexico or the tribes of East Africa, all refer to God's power unleashed, matched by nothing else on Earth.

$$\int\!\!\int\!\!\int$$

The landscape is still rolling and arid, punctuated by an occasional Masai settlement, a ring of circular huts around a cattle enclosure surrounded at night by thorny brush to keep out lions and other predators.

The weaver bird nests hang like tassels from the trees and swing in the breeze, festive yet doleful. The male creates the residence, his mate must approve it, or it will be discarded and he must begin again.

The termite mounds cling to the roots of the acacias they have strangled or which were dead when they began their remarkable architectural adventure. These two species are enough to silence the skeptics who insist that humanity alone, of all the creatures on earth, is the only one to communicate, to build, to create, to reason, to fall and then to rise again.

We pass clusters, like feather dusters, of young Masai in black. These are boys at puberty who have just endured circumcision. In a few weeks, when they heal, they can wear the red of the adults and join the clan. Meantime, they earn a little cash offering themselves for photographs to the cars passing on their way to the farms in the increasingly fertile land, or on to Arusha, Tanzania's fourth-largest city.

The nation of Tanzania, Eliud explains, dates formally from 1964, when it was created from the much larger mainland territory of Tanganyika, part of German East Africa from the 1880's to 1919, when the British took it from them by a mandate of the League of Nations following the First World War, fought as keenly and as earnestly here as in Europe. What had been a rich but unruly, uneven and pestilential territory was joined politically to the coastal archipelago of Zanzibar, originally a Portuguese colony that came under the jurisdiction of the Sultanate of Oman, followed by the British protectorate at the end of the nineteenth century. Its temporal and spiritual leader ruled as an Ottoman Sultan, who despite the watchful eye of the British Consulate and the blind eye turned by the many Christian missions, moderated the slave trade and procured supplies and bearers for the explorers who from the key island headed inland due west in search of the source of the Nile River, the last great geographic prize on earth.

Later the fledgling country served as a military outpost during the Second World War, providing munitions and soldiers. The one-time intention, during the immediate post-war years, was an East African Federation, to include Kenya, Uganda and Tanzania, but the project failed to prosper, in part because the British had created an assiduous system of civil service and public administration yet this was applied unevenly. Tiny Uganda, for example, had something like one hundred and twenty-eight post offices while vast Tanzania had virtually none, and if there were any, they never, says Eliud, worked very well. So the plans for an integrated political entity ended in discord, Eliud assures us, mostly because no one ever received his mail, and never on time.

After Independence from Britain in 1961 Tanzania chose to follow the policies of the murdered ideologue and Africa's still beloved Julius Nyerere, into a very sincere but ineffectual socialism, while Uganda went for a power structure, and this fell apart under the cruelty and intransigence of Idi Amín: (see: *The Last King of Scotland*, directed by Kevin Macdonald, 2006, a very effective film, with an Oscar for a terrorific Forrest Whittiker.)

Kenya, meanwhile, went capitalist and has been held together, during and since Jomo Kenyatta, by the European and North American powers that require her success and survival. All three territories were incredibly rich in natural resources: gems, metals, coffee, tea, fine quality mineral water, lumber, fishing, leather, animal products, grains and tropical fruits among others, but none of this came to much, especially in Tanzania, which even tried putting in a sisal crop, encouraged in the seventies by Mexico's erratic President Luis Echeverría, but is now committed to receiving support from conservationist groups around the world and, of course, adventure tourism, in order to survive.

𝄞

Tawny eagles pluck their prey from a burned-off area near the highway. A family of eight or ten giraffes watches us in graceful tolerance before lumbering on. The land has changed very quickly, as has our altitude, in a remarkably short distance. There is much evidence of wind erosion. Then the landscape is transformed again. Now we are surrounded by rolling knolls and, just as suddenly, by luxuriant agriculture shaded by eucalyptus and pepper trees: bananas, corn, squash, beans, coffee, sisal, and breathy lilac jacaranda, in euphoric seasonal bloom. The round thatched huts in clusters surrounded by maguey have turned into orderly communities devoted to cultivation. We approach Arusha, a colorful and dilapidated frontier town much like Nairobi must have been several decades ago. Population: one hundred and forty thousand.

We settle down to lunch at the "New Arusha Hotel" in the center of town. It lies in a fertile garden, off limits to the chunky women swathed in bright cloth, sauntering along the street with buckets and parcels on their heads; or the goats and bicycles; or the safari-hawkers trying to find an adventure-hungry tourist ripe for a bargain.

The shops up and down the side streets peddle everything from zebra skins to boots to wood carving to necklaces confected of camel's teeth. Film is expensive and bottled mineral water in plastic containers costs six U.S. dollars a liter, a small fortune when considered in the context of the local economy at that time. Eliud, bless him, has anticipated this and carries a case of bottled water, to last during our stay in his country, at the lodges in the game parks not otherwise supplied.

We are met at lunch by the A&K representative in Arusha, who double-checks our progress and answers our questions. He is tall, lean, extraordinarily beautiful, with refined features and a good education. He was born in Rwanda and was ecstatic when he saw I had heard of it. "But how could I not?" I asked him, "after George Schaller's exceptional study of the mountain gorilla and the on-site research done by Dian Fossey?" He was loquacious after that. We talked about Michael Apted's 1988 film, *Gorillas in the Mist.* Trouble was already brewing in Rwanda, civil war came in 1994; it hardly boded well for the survival of the gorillas, or in fact any other wildlife in the region. The human loss was also monumental. There are no reliable records for either.

$$\int\!\!\int\!\!\int$$

Then we left Arusha, of the engine repair shops, the grain exchanges, the post office where people have their mail sent to a box number, the markets and beauty shops—where the women come either to have their hair straightened or to be sculpted into tiny braids which in turn are braided again until the head is a stylized cap under the broiling sun—and we continue to descend.

We are travelling along a new highway in construction, an Italian contribution intended to link Arusha and the then capital of the country, the drab Dar es Salaam on the coast, to the intended, but unfulfilled, project of a new capital, Dodoma, four hundred miles away. Farms occupy the niches in the rolling landscape. After the brief and fertile tropical pocket, erosion again appears on the land and the country, visibly part of the Rift Valley, is arid.

None of this matters to the Masai, with their singular notion of time and the Universe, but it indeed affects the tribes and the class structure in the modern dimension. To the Masai time conforms to a cycle according to the seasons. Clocks and calendars and closed-in places do not fit in their world. They are governed by natural accommodation, not by accomplishment or achievement, certainly not by Western standards. They have no notion of success or failure. If there is a drought or a wet spell it makes no difference. If the crops come to fruition or cease to produce it can only be a passing action, hardly significant in the overall scheme. On the other hand, any alteration of this concept, any interference from the outside, and their mind just stops. They lose the sense of transition and therefore assume that whatever is happening will never change, that it will have to be endured forever, however long that might be. What is religion, anyway, but a relationship of moral, cultural and traditional values, which assume a part of the responsibility in a man's priorities, within his society, to let him know what is expected of him. If these values also bind him to a part of his history and tell him what happens after he dies, his problems are solved. Eliud is very clear on this. "Everything else is either manipulation or blackmail."

We are fully in the Rift Valley now, that persistent geological vein that rips vertically into eastern Africa, rupturing eight thousand kilometers with a fault line whose heat and movement have served to press and preserve the remains of earliest mankind as well as his antecedents. More of this when we reach the Olduvai Gorge.

We cross a village whose name, translated, means "Mosquito Creek", a bit of lazy, remote Papaloapan on the coastal plain of Veracruz, where Tomás spent part of his infancy, and we make a mental note to stop here on our way back.

Now we begin to climb, above the lakes of Manyara, to which we will also return. Baboons line the road and beg for sweets as we pass. They watch us balefully from the shadow of the baobab trees, those gigantic tangled clumps, like skeins of yarn gone mad or roots upside down, that will always remind us of **The Little Prince**. We are driving fast and the road is terrible. Eliud believes that the worse the road the faster one should go because, he says, that way the van flies from crest to crest, "from bump to bump", instead of sinking into the potholes. It is on a smoothly paved road that one may drive slowly.

We are also in a hurry. We have to make the rangers' cabin at the entrance to Ngorongoro Conservation Area before six o'clock, or be shut out for the night. We catch our first and fleeting glimpse of the "Big Hole", twenty kilometers in diameter, a shadowy bowl of enormous proportions and sinuous contours, the ancient crater grown over and dark.

We penetrate the mounting gloom of the rain forest that lines the crater's rim. The mist is as dense as the night, lit only by the glow from the outrageous October moon that disguises the inverted constellations. We are below the Equator. A chill invades the van, deceptive and cloying, fingers of cold that reach across the ferns and the lianas and clutch our feet and legs, erasing the heat and the dust of a very long day.

We arrive at the Ngorongoro Crater Lodge, whose main building lurches against the edge of the crater while the cabins stretch across a dark field in a crooked line. We are told to keep to the paths in case the buffalo are wandering: everyone knows the Cape buffalo is the most dangerous animal in Africa. So wrote Hemingway, so claimed Broor Blixen, every scout and guide, the hunter and the hunted, and so we would learn for ourselves.

We threw our gear into the log cabin with the open cracks through which the cold seeped. A water heater supplied the tub but there was no shower head so a squatting rinse was the best we could hope for, without really stripping and settling in—not likely. Light is dim, except for the moon. The mist is silent, but for the dainty pattering of a cat's paws on the shingled roof. We add a padded vest to the khaki costume, rescue the hair from a day under the Australian Outback hat, change neckerchiefs and traipse gingerly, barely aided by a reticent flashlight, toward the terrace, with its dining hall. It all has the feel of a ski lodge and is equally fraternal. The lounge is decorated with an orderly row of horns, and when we stop to study them the waiter immediately challenges us to identify them, from the diminutive dik-dik to the Thomson's and Grant's gazelles, oryx, spring bok, waterbuck, wildebeest, hardibeest, on up to the stately eland, the largest of the antelopes. There were also buffalo horns, behind the bar.

The dining room was full but the staff took the time to be very attentive, their rapt attention barely disguised under their formal exterior. They could hardly contain their curiosity. "Where is Mexico?" We tried to explain, even to drawing a map in my notebook. "Is yours a Commonwealth country?"

TUESDAY, OCTOBER 17

Down to the crater, in a four-wheel drive Jeep, driven by Charles, a boy who might have been younger than Eliud, but he had none of our driver's finesse or knowledge of the wild life. Eliud traveled with a full library, and could discourse equally on birds, mammals and plants, as well as on the people of the region. Charles simply kept the car on the rutted dirt road and with street-smart shrewdness knew how to swing across the lanes inside the crater, and to best find the animals. He kept his opinions to himself.

Pursuing a lion on the prowl, harassing zebra and wildebeest or ferreting out a solitary elephant at its bath is not my idea of enjoying Africa but it is certainly an improvement over the days of the White Hunter and in any case there is always the challenge, to see what you can get on film through the dust, sudden bumps in the road, across the distance and despite the traffic from the other vehicles, eager to provide their clients with the same thrill. Thrills mean tips.

This was long before the advent of digital cameras. I had chosen for the trip the simplest of automatic cameras with a standard reflex lens, just to prove you need no heavy gear or elaborate interchangeable lenses. By the time you get all the expensive equipment in focus or find the right lens—unless you are Joan and Allan Root—the less complicated the better. The Roots pioneered nature documentaries and their work has never been surpassed. They took incredible chances, were indifferent to danger, but produced the goods. Alan was born in 1937 in London, and was making amateur films when the two met. Joan was born in Nairobi in 1936, daughter of Edmund Thorpe, a British banker who immigrated to Kenya, "to start a new life", and became a successful coffee planter and safari guide.

While Alan worked on *Gorillas in the Mist* an enraged gorilla bit his thigh. In 1969 he lost a finger to the bite of a deadly puff adder. In spite of it all the marriage lasted two decades and produced a dozen films, yet ultimately the union succumbed to the pressure and was dissolved. Joan moved to the Lake Naivasha region of Kenya, and in the last years of her life, like many other white or European landowners, was subjected to threats and harassment yet refused to leave. After a burglary in September of 2005 she had steel doors installed on each side of her bedroom, which already had bars on the windows.

Five days before her seventieth birthday, in 2006, Joan Root was murdered by four men who came to her door carrying AK-47's. There were many suspects: disgruntled former employees, criminal gangs, organized crime rackets, poachers, those whose economic interests were threatened by her activism on behalf of restricted fishing in the lake and even Task Force members. The four men, evidently contract killers, who were arrested and charged with her murder, pleaded not guilty and were acquitted in August 2007. No one ever learned who had hired them.

First we saw a pride of fat, very satisfied lions. The sun was high in the sky so we had come along far past their breakfast time. The buffalo were at their grazing, though the grass was sparse at this time of year, just before the rains. We came across a large herd of zebra with their inevitable companions, the wildebeest. One grazes close to the roots and the other takes just the tip of the grass; one has a better sense of smell and the other keener eyesight; both are gifted at skirting the ill or elderly in their midst so the predators have a prize and the rest run free: they stick together, well-chosen friends.

Despite the proximity of the lions the gazelles and the other grazing animals feed unalarmed. They know the lions are already satisfied and, in any case, as long as no one breaks the barrier of tolerance—a distance of about thirty meters—there is room for everyone, even within the confines of the crater. Coming closer, however, means danger so it also means trouble and the herds amble off until the limits are again established. Men love war but would do well to evolve enough to heed the rules of the animal kingdom.

A male lion shrouded by a clump of tall grass, dozing, occasionally lifts his magnificent head, then lays it down again. His cubs sprawl near his gigantic paws. Behind him a herd of zebra-wildebeest lumbers across the plain. The Blacksmith Plover plies his trade and the crowned cranes caw into the wind; two herons stretch their long necks; a solitary jackal moves into the grass and disappears; a hyena vanishes into the watershed; ibis, spoonbill, finch and busy stilts crowd the edges of a water hole. It is a very orderly world, perfectly balanced and in absolute harmony. A lioness stalks across the grass to get a closer look at us, sees no danger and moves away.

We approach the alkaline rim of a flat lake. Thousands of flamingoes take to the air at our approach, in a pink, fluttering cloud with no beginning or end. Their pale reflection on the water is rippled by a fresh breeze. The herds stand near the water, sniffing the wind, they separate, then come together again. The so carefully choreographed ballet continues through the morning.

A swampy area: a clump of hippos with pale pink eyes raise their heads to glare at the cruising ducks, then lumber off through the elephant grass. Hippos spend the daylight hours, if possible, submerged in the brooks, swamps and pools, then come out to hunt in the cool of the evening, to avoid sunburn. They are surprisingly agile despite the dumpy little legs and the huge, cumbersome body, named by Herodotus: "the river horse". In the water they are completely in control and can be deadly dangerous, especially if a swimmer or another animal chances by and gets caught in one of their private disputes. Even the crocodiles keep them at a distance, unless there happens to be a baby, separated from the rest.

An elephant cow nurses her calf among the water lilies, her ears flapping at our approach. She is warning us to keep our distance. Hearing the sound her relatives approach, and close ranks around her. Gestation period for a female is eighteen months, for a male twenty-two. A baby elephant at birth weighs up to eight hundred kilos. The world's largest land mammal must also consume anywhere from seventy to three hundred kilos of vegetation per head every day, and drink eighty to two hundred and forty liters of water, with great quantities required as well for bathing. He is happy with both dust and mud, effective sun blocks; these are hard to supply simultaneously and so elephants keep to the shade during the hot daytime hours, to avoid sunburn, and their enormous ears, flapping softly, serve as air-conditioning.

2.

A DISDAINFUL ELEPHANT

A full grown bull may join a bachelor club but will return to the herd to visit his females. His life span ranges from sixty to seventy years. He weighs anywhere from three to six tons. He likes his privacy, his mud, time for meditation and a quiet rhythm to his life, though he is more agile than he appears and can attain great speed if provoked. He is a devoted family man and both cows and bulls collaborate in the raising of the young. This is a community effort, in fact, and the older calves also help with the younger, as would be the case in any extended family. The smaller children are naughty, the older are mischievous, the adolescents are stubborn, at times, in fact, insufferable. All of this is clearly visible through the binoculars, while we stand in our car, literally for hours, observing the herds from a distance of about fifty meters.

The secretary birds, cocky, disdainful, open paths in the grass on the trail of the snakes they feed on. They are named for the flopping feathers around their heads, said to look like the pencils behind a stenographer's ears, though in actual fact they are "serpent eagles", and so are termed in Spanish or French.

We stumbled across a black rhino cow with her calf on a dusty knoll. She bounded to her feet as we approached but kept her distance. There are few if any rhinos left in the wild but back then there might have been about four thousand. They are nearsighted yet have an acute sense of smell and can charge like an express train. The black rhino is less ugly than his cousin, the white rhino, the name in fact a derivation of the true designation, "wide", to describe not the color but rather the outsized jaws.

We depart for a picnic area near a lake, at first glance idyllic, with Vervet monkeys chattering from the trees, baboons that leap out of the grass to poise on dry stumps and a male bushbuck that bounds through the wood like "the afternoon of the faun", until we hear of the black "kite" birds, fierce vultures with their beaks and talons like knives, that plunge toward an innocent lunch to snatch a bite from the lips, or better still, to make off with the food right out of our mouths. They can cut off a nose with a single swipe. We think better of the plan and take our box lunch into the Jeep.

For some this is a watery paradise, in fact a camp site for people who choose tents as opposed to our cabins on the crater rim. There are flowers here, the first we have seen, yellow and alive, among the dead trunks and the lacy silhouette of the copses of acacias of the same hue, known as the "yellow-fever" or "yellow jack" acacia, at one time thought to be the cause of that acute viral hemorrhage, before the *Aedes aegypti* and other species of mosquitoes were known. In the eighteenth and nineteenth centuries, while European explorers quested after the sources of rivers and colonialism mapped Africa, the many fevers—malaria, yellow fever and others— were termed "miasmas", attributed indeed to the swamps of Africa and the Americas, where they thrived, but not to Asia, which had other, unrelated diseases, not caused by the bite of the female of these specific strains of mosquito.

Even in the best of circumstances this is not a park for a Sunday drive or an outing with the children, though many come. We, like the other visitors whose cars crowd around ours, have covered some eighty kilometers today, round and round, driving up and down, burning up fuel and pursuing the beasts at their business or pleasure. The licensed drivers know where to go and how to keep their clients inside the cars. There is no hunting here, and no exploring on foot. Ngorongoro is maintained as an ecosystem with funds provided by institutions around the world, initially promoted by Bernhard Grzimek and his son Michael, who crashed his plane near here. His monument stands on the rim of the crater, just above us.

WEDNESDAY, OCTOBER 18

After another night on the rim and an early breakfast we depart with Eliud along the road away from the crater and into the park beyond. Moss and lianas quickly change to scrub and acacia, to thorns and dust. We start stripping off layers of clothes, back down to the long-sleeved shirt, the rough pants, the well-designed light weight athletic shoes, the thermal aerobics socks, a scarf of lightweight Indian cotton, under the indispensable hat. Clothing in Africa is military khaki or fatigue green, to attract the least attention of the presumably color-blind animals. White is out.

We are on our way to *Asirenget* or Serengeti, "the endless plains", fourteen thousand seven hundred square kilometers in all, but between the Ngorongoro Crater and the entrance to Serengeti Park is a vast, thirsty expanse broken only by the mirage on the horizon. The occasional acacia woods, inhabited by giraffe and a skeleton or two beside the road, are the only signs of habitation of any kind.

Eliud suddenly turns off the bumpy graded road to lurch into a mad dash across the dusty plain itself, scattering a pair—black male, brown female—of ostrich on our way. Through the dust we can barely make out the trail of the wildebeest across the sweeping landscape, in a forlorn line like a hairline thread on its endless and compelling annual migration, loping across the desolate lunar undulations. Over a million wildebeest start out on the journey, which takes an entire year. Along the way the herd crosses fields, forests, woods and plains, fords rivers in flood, gives birth and discards its dead. The migration may swell to two and a half million but will be reduced to its original numbers, hardier and stronger than ever, when it returns to its starting point, after making a circuit from the Ngorongoro, up into the northern expanse of the Serengeti on the Tanzania side, known as the Masai Mara or "freckled plain" on the Kenya side, then back again, down through the Serengeti.

The mind wanders as it dwells on the wisdom of nature, then comes back sharply at the sight of a family of giraffe only ten or so meters away. We continue on the dusty track, with no road and a perfect chance of bogging down. A bucking adolescent giraffe turns to stare at us, while its parents, patient and attentive, wait for him.

A dry wash becomes dull green, at the unexpected appearance of sisal-like plants called *oldupai*, a Masai word to describe "the place of the sisal". The name had been mispronounced by a German butterfly hunter named Cartwinkle, who arrived here in 1911. We have reached a small building, a wooden house which serves as a museum, and a thatched shelter that is the look-out over a deep gorge, ochre and red, with a rounded hill behind it. This is Olduvai Gorge, read about it all my life, where it is said that Man was born. I was moved to tears while I paced along the rim, too touched to listen to Eliud and Michael, our guide, one of the workers with the team of paleoanthropologists who excavate during the season and earn tips from the tourists. He is rambling. Or is he? I must pay attention and return to my notes.

It seems the Gorge originally produced the remains of the extinct pachyderm *dinothaerium,* a fact quickly reported to the paleontological museum in Berlin. Remember, this was German East Africa. Kaiser Wilhelm II himself gave his personal support to an expedition in 1913 under geologist Hans Reck, who remained in the field for three months. He collected fossils here which included fragments of what was determined to be *Homo sapiens,* our specific human progenitor. A skeleton then tested by Carbon 14 was dated to seventeen thousand B.C. Another brick in the wall. Yet the riddles persisted.

A note here about dates. It has become fashionable in academic circles to replace "B.C." with "B.C.E." (*Before the Christian Era).* The indications for A.D. then become "Christian Era". In view of the fact that no one knows with any certainty when, exactly, the Christian Era began, or the precise date of birth of Jesus Christ, and the only available dates were arbitrarily assigned at the order of Constantine the Great at the first Nicaean Council in the fourth century, and since religions other than the Christian can equally claim an era as their own, I will retain the academic classics and my dating will remain B.C. and A.D. If I refer to a millennium it will be "B.C." Otherwise I am automatically referring to A.D. Islamic dates will also be registered as A.D. though I thoroughly respect the Hegira. If I needed to refer to Hindu or Buddhist dates, though I am just as devoted to these faiths, I would also use "B.C." and "A.D." Old habits are hard to break.

In 1928 the British archeologist, naturalist and paleoanthropologist Dr. Louis Seymour Bazette Leakey visited Berlin as a tourist. He examined Reck's findings and was convinced that Olduvai could yield considerably more, if the excavations were pursued. He organized his legendary expedition in 1931 and worked here until 1959 before he, and his wife Mary, stumbled on the "Southern Ape", *Australopithecus boiseion,* on July 17. It had been twenty-eight years. Leakey, though a devout Christian, was obsessed with Charles Darwin, and resolutely sustained the notion of an "African Genesis" of mankind. The South African Raymond Dart had discovered other remains in southern Africa in 1911, but "Boisie" was the first finan-cially supported find and therefore officially accredited.

Zinj, an ancient Arabic word for East Africa, was associated with another find, *Zinjanthropus,* thus combining a Greek word for Man, and applying it to remains dating from one a half million years ago. In 1960 another specie, *Homo habilis*, about 1.6 million years old and with an articulated thumb, was discovered and identified. In 1963 the Leakeys isolated *Homo erectus,* an upright ancestor, about 1.5 million years old, and identified this "walking ape" among the many sites along the Gorge.

The main Olduvai Gorge runs about fifty-five kilometers across the barren countryside, with a side gorge jutting off another forty-five kilometers. In 1978 Mary Leakey, by this time a widow working with her son Richard, discovered the fossilized footprints presum-ably belonging to the earliest known species, a common ancestor of ape and man, making us therefore cousins. *Australopithecus afa-rensis* was named for Afar, the region in southern Ethiopia where these fossils were unearthed. They are calculated to be 3.6 million years old.

Meanwhile, however, my friend Donald Carl Johanson, born in Chicago of Swedish descendance with degrees from the University of Illinois and the University of Chicago, was actually working in the Afar Triangle of the Hadar region, along the rift in Ethiopia, and on November 24, 1974, together with Maurice Taieb and Yves Doppens, discovered a hip bone and other fossil fragments of a female hominid, and changed forever the course of paleoanthropol-ogy. "The radio was playing *Lucy in the Sky With Diamonds,* under a dazzling African desert night, and so we named her 'Lucy' and it was magical. Lucy is estimated to be about 3.2 million years old and currently resides in the Natural History Museum of New York, but her legacy is beyond calculation."

In 1986 Donald Johanson made another discovery, of a skeleton of the oldest known *Homo habilis,* 1.8 million years. He considers her to be Lucy's younger sister. She was found here, in the gorge at Olduvai. We saw no work in progress, unfortunately, and had to wait until a luncheon in Cuernavaca, in Mexico, many years later, for Don to recount the details, and the emotion, of a find of this magnitude.

The digging season is from July to September, during the dry period. It is presumed that two million years ago Olduvai was an alkaline lakebed, which very likely disappeared about a million and a half years ago, as a result of seismic activity in the Rift Valley. Since then streams from the highlands dug chasms about one hundred meters deep to form the Gorge, and so preserving the ancient formations that held the fossils rooted in the cross section.

There are five different strata in the Gorge. Black volcanic rock, the lava flows and basalt of about two million years ago, complement the whitish volcanic ash on the slope, that dates from about 1.9 to 1.6 million years ago. "Boisie" and "Habilis" were found in this first level.

The second level lies underneath a red outcropping that revealed "Erectus", dating from 1.5 million to 900,000 years ago. The Red Level conforms to a dry and arid climate prevalent about eight hundred to five hundred thousand years ago, when there were no stone tools and no physical remains. The gray strata above the red represent the fourth level, *Homo erectus* again, but around four hundred to two hundred thousand years ago. The top level, or most recent, dates from one hundred thousand to seventeen thousand years B.C. and in paleontological terms is "modern", equivalent to *Homo sapiens*.

We question Don Johanson: Did humans originate in Africa and then migrate to other parts of the globe. "Yes," he replies unequivocally, "yet the jury is not in. It never is, until the next discovery proves it wrong."

Question: "When did Man become Human?"

Reply: "As soon as he took up stone or bone tools and held them in his hands and used them. Initially, we imagine, he used them to protect himself, that is to destroy any competitor for the animals he hunted for food. Aggression is built in, his survival kit. He ultimately regimented this, and has been doing so ever since."

$$\mathint{\int\!\!\int\!\!\int}$$

The geologist and anthropologist John P. Paresso is now at work here, or was while we were in Olduvai. We took a few minutes to go through the small museum and to glance through the selection of Masai beads and jewelry, of no consequence, except to realize, as we watched the Masai coming up the gorge with their cattle, or the women shunting down the path with their bundles on their heads, that Man is still here and probably always will be, oblivious to the scientific speculation far, far away, regarding his antiquity, where he came from or how he got there. This is of very little importance with regard to the foraging of the cattle or the appearance of water. "One stays alive as long as possible," says Dr. Paresso. "The rest does not really concern us."

We again cross the dusty plain, disturbing the same family of giraffe in passing, then we move down the road toward the mirage. If Tanzania is rough, with a minimum of hydroelectric stations or pipelines, housing developments or factories, perhaps it's better this way.

We pass under the portal that divides the Ngorongoro Conservation Area from Serengeti Game Park and soon we detect the first of the rocky lumps that rise off the flat plain. They are called *kopjes,* at this latitude pronounced "cop gees", an Africaans word for "outcropping", mindless of the Dutch "j" which is pronounced as in "I". The jutting rocks are properly termed "cope-ees", and serve as a microcosmic world, complete with plants, animals, insects, often even water.

There are now trees on the land, huge clumps of prickly-pear, low brush and, at the rangers' station, "Superb" starlings by the thousands. That is, by the way, their true name. Their iridescent blue and gleaming purple feathers flutter in the sun against the deep blue of the sky, as they chatter, lurch after picnickers' crumbs and plunder the remains abandoned by a group of Spanish tourists. They are greedy, these gorgeous birds, dazzling, among the most beautiful on earth.

"Ostrich at nine o'clock", shouts Eliud.

"Mirage at three o'clock," replies Tomás. We begin to talk like *Top Gun*, very much the hit of the day, but it saves time and pinpoints the things to look for, as we scan the horizon with our binoculars and madly scribble notes.

Kori bustard "at seven o'clock". Jackal "at ten o'clock", lurking in a clump of dry grass, with a watchful eye on the gazelle prancing by. A dozen or more ostrich strung out on the right, "at two o'clock". We are now inside the National Park. Endless plains, indeed.

Men by the road are working on a rusted bulldozer. At a distance, the outline of buzzards near a carcass. Topi, gazelles, zebras, more ostrich. And the wart hog, tail up like a flag, round firm rump, prancing like a deformed pony, deadly and delightful. "At eleven o'clock", a dappled giraffe in dappled light, forelegs splayed out to drink from a steam half-hidden in the grass. If it failed to spread those legs it would choke to death.

Against sweeping light and sporadic curtains of rain, on the edge of a knoll, barely visible, a numberless caravan of gazelle in silhouette, accented with the outline of the acacias. Far to one side, the thunderous sky melting from soft blue to angry steel gray. A mist begins to gather in the low spots until it looks like a bay on a great sea, framed by a pair of *kopjes*. A giraffe with her baby contemplates the approaching pair of increasingly rare cheetahs stalking a handful of gazelle on the opposite knoll. They make their ninety-kilometer-per-hour charge but the gazelles change course in midair. The cheetahs miss their supper. Perhaps they were only rehearsing a diversion.

Two or three giraffes stalk along in a line like pilgrims bound for a shrine. A solitary light plane circles to land. The day is waning and the mosquitoes start to bite. We are about to turn back, to check into the Seronera Lodge, when the impervious grass, too thin and wan to hide even a rat, suddenly parts to reveal a magnificent leopard, first the head, then the emerging muscular machine of a body, the long graceful tail, the striding, disdainful legs. So much for the assumption that nothing could be hiding in the grass.

She ignores us and stops only long enough to urinate, a pejorative statement at best. A traffic jam ensues. Every car in the Seronera Woodland has converged to get a look at her. How did they know? "They use their walkie-talkies", says Eliud, as if we were mentally defective. There is no sound. Everyone is holding his breath while he or she trains binoculars on the insolent spotted backside. It is too late in the day for cameras and she knows it. Then she moves off across the grass, beyond a stream, the white tuft on the tail like a banner. The zebra, confused, run in the darkening afternoon straight toward her, then veer off in another direction. I can smell the damp earth, the moist grass, the webs of the leaves in the trees and the pungent stench of feline, disappearing into the dusk. The evening is closing in against a silver sky, which flares pink along the edges.

There are bumps in the road. *Pole* means "sorry". We are waiting for Eliud to utter an apology for the jolt but none is forthcoming. *Pole-pole* means slowly. We try both. Eliud ignores us. Too late in the day.

The lodge is dramatic, of huge wooden beams and massive picture windows, set into a large *kopje*. There are hyrax in the open hall, mongoose in the garden and baboon on the boulders outside the dining room. The residential wing was designed by formula, with standard rooms, nothing spectacular—disappointing after the splendid lobby—but we are warned to keep the windows closed to keep the baboons out. There is a bathroom and the tub has a shower head but there is no hot water. No drinking water, either, at any price but Eliud has seen to bringing our own. There is electric light from dusk to midnight, which allows the screening of a Joan and Alan Root nature documentary after dinner, with tea in the lounge. Snatches of conversation among the other guests: "Did you get an elephant?" "No, but we got a leopard and two cheetahs." "Did you see the wart hogs?" "The baboon in my picture got away and I missed the giraffe crossing the road, went out of focus, but it was a great day!" We got all of those and still managed to visit Olduvai. We feel infinitely superior.

THURSDAY, OCTOBER 19

Dawn breaks suddenly, with the grunting of the lions, harsh and rasping, while they stalk their breakfast. The agama lizards, bright scarlet and iridescent blue-violet, share the rocks with the hyrax, crouching and suspicious. I can hear the hoofed animals rustling in the grass. The morning is borne on the clacking, cackling, twitter and chatter of a thousand birds and the patter of monkeys in the trees.

There are baboons on the roof and clinging to the contours of the *kopje*, not unlike the rocky den of Susannah York and Stewart Whitman in Cy Endfield's 1965 *Sands of the Kalahari,* when Whitman challenges the alpha baboon that threatens them; he fights and wins and becomes, himself, the alpha of the pack, a lesson in ethology, the science of behavior, since the social structure of the baboon is the nearest in nature to that of the human.

As the sun rises higher in the sky Eliud removes the top of the car for game viewing. Other vehicles are equipped with a top on folding legs, like a card table's; the hat and neckerchief are essentials of the wardrobe. We wander the trails, observe the animals, take our pictures, make our notes, until we are finally well out on the plain, when Eliud suddenly decides to leave the road, furtively of course, as this is totally forbidden in all the parks but the Mara. He wants to check, he says, on three lionesses sunning themselves among the acacias on a *kopje.* The rangers could follow our tracks and Eliud is visibly altered, but not enough to return to the assigned paths. We tell him not to do this, that for us it is unnecessary and that we have no wish to break the rules. Does he think this will garner a larger tip? He smiles to himself, a cunning smirk that we catch in the rear-view mirror, as he almost smashes into a lone Thomson's gazelle lying half-hidden in the grass, its feet tucked up under itself. At our approach it turns to move away and we see that it is lame. It will end its day on a lion's or a leopard's or a cheetah's dinner table. And so, perhaps, will we.

Serengeti, the park and the work done here in conservation, owe a great debt to Bernhard Grzimek and his son Michael, whose monument we had seen in Ngorongoro. Thanks to their campaigning the Frankfurt Zoological Society contributed planes, boots, uniforms and equipment to assist Tanzania's government in protecting its wildlife and encouraging severe sanctions against poachers. The sanctions extend to tourists who don't behave themselves.

Many species, however, despite the efforts on their behalf, are nearly extinct in the wild. Most curious is the plight of the cheetah, the only large cat that can be completely domesticated yet remains the most delicate and difficult to breed in captivity, a strategy originally undertaken, successfully as it happens, by naturalist Gerald Durrell at his sanctuary in Jersey, in Britain's Channel Islands.

So many males have been killed off, mostly for coats or bedspreads, that cubs born in the wild were genetic brothers and inbreeding killed them off. Since then a joint program has been devised, among Tanzania, Kenya and Zimbabwe, to attempt to import genetically diverse males from the zoos and game parks of the world, to fortify the gene pool and return specimens to their source or deliver them, following Joy Adamson's example, into the wild.

Our day ends opposite a herd of quiet impala, deceptively similar to deer, that collectively launch themselves into a single leap, change course in midair and head off, like a school of fish, in the opposite direction, but not before several of their numbers are sacrificed for the game barbecue in the hotel garden and subsequently the dinner table. Would I also lose my appetite if these were beef or chicken?

FRIDAY, OCTOBER 20

After breakfast next to the ladies who had just been to what was then known as Zaïre (now the Democratic Republic of Congo) and the Australian couple who arrived yesterday from Botswana, we took off toward Manyara.

About two hundred meters up the road, the car broke down. Eliud had checked it, but it could be anything. Though human beings on foot are the forbidden fruit of the game parks, he asks us to get down and "behave ourselves", while he changes the tire, takes a look at the spark plugs and sees what else it might be. I claim to have to use the bathroom in order to have a walk back to the hotel, thinking to myself that at last I have a chance at a photo of the wart hog just up the way, or the baby giraffe just ahead. Now who's breaking the rules?

And here I am, alone against nature, in the middle of nowhere though the hotel is around the corner; and I would be loathe to trade places with Burton and Speke, or Stanley or Livingstone or Hemingway the Hunter. I am ten meters tall, invincible and cunning. I look all around as I stalk down the road and there is nothing, no threat at all. Why are the rangers so strict? The land is barren. Detecting an animal in the brush is no problem at all.

Without warning I see three large shadows out of the corner of one eye. The shadows are moving, even snorting. I can see the light on the lowered dark horns and the eyes are red with fire. One gigantic hoof scuffs at the dirt before settling down to really pawing the earth in preparation for a charge. Three Cape buffalo, disturbed at their morning nap. Do not run, I say to myself. Do not change pace. Continue moving, at the same speed, in the same direction. This is the most dangerous animal in Africa but panic is the worst enemy. They have no more business with you, I comfort myself, than you with them. They are neither wounded nor yet enraged.

And so it was. It took what seemed to be several years, but I reached the hotel, as chagrined and pouting as the day of the bomb at the airport in Paris. The three buffalo returned to their nap. The periphery of the hotel, I tell myself, is just as good a place to explore. Wart hogs charge and baby giraffes have parents so I would be better off at the rear of the lodge, around the garbage dump, where the fabulous marabou storks flutter and cluster in the trees, waving their gorgeous plumes, and the sly hyena gapes from the bush to see if I am a competitor or simply a curiosity seeker.

A boy from the kitchen saunters by, with a wheel barrow full of empty glass bottles, to dump on the already overflowing heap of cans and glass in the oil drums by the garbage. With extreme difficulty we manage to communicate, but it takes awhile. I ask why these people never thought of returning the glass and metal to Arusha for recycling, instead of adding more debris to the bush.

I realize the excessive zeal in the approach but it has to start someplace. There is no question of an argument. The boy is amazed by the idea. He calls a number of his co-workers over and we continue the conversation, always laboring against the language barrier (though English is the country's official *lingua franca)*, to try to explain about recycling, processing, different applications of what novelist Sidney Sheldon called "The accumulated excretia of man's plastic existence", in order to avoid the contamination and the eyesore, as well as the dangers to man and beast, of the glass and metal in the dump. There was no point in taking the matter further and the idea of a compost was out of the question. It's now more than a quarter of a century later and the idea is only beginning to gain momentum.

It was all very entertaining and potentially productive until Eliud sent word that the car was ready, which it was not. We managed to drive to "the village", not a village at all but a petrol pump on the *kopje,* behind the little museum, where again I get down from the car to snoop about. A small snake slithers by, narrow, metallic brown and shiny, definitely non-poisonous. How can I be so sure? I stumble on a covey of civets. No point trying to follow them, they have escaped to a copse of formidable thorn bushes, the spikes a good six or eight centimeters in length. Nothing to be gained there, not even a photograph.

More delays. We return to the lodge, which gives me the chance to write a treatise on recycling for the suggestion box. Eliud, meantime, has taken the car to the rangers' garage in search of parts or some kind of help. The drivers may share a tip on the walkie-talkie as to the location of one or another animal but they are little inclined to help each other with mechanical advice or automobile parts, other than a report, if given the opportunity, when a car is in trouble. We need a condenser. If Eliud fails to find one he will install an old one he happens to have on hand, "and then we pray", he says, with feigned enthusiasm. He is very worried.

I climb up through the ascending wooden walkways to the top of the *kopje,* behind the lounge. Here I have time to study the view across the plain: lizards, monkeys, hyrax and civets, from the vantage point of this granite island on a sea of grass and dust, surrounded by soft trees, sisal plants and the pensive baboons.

11:30 a.m. We are finally underway. The sun is high and we have to cross the "mirage plain" with its clouds of dust and washboard road. We come across hundreds and hundreds of zebra, all moving toward a single spot where they seem to be massing. They are not equine, as many people suppose, but rather the African version of the Asian ass. They are donkeys! Groups of two, heads on each other's withers, clusters of three or four, slow caravans of a dozen, but all seemingly called to convene at a pre-arranged site.

They are accompanied by a few ostrich, an occasional topi or wart hog. We are now crossing the open grassland, greenish gold and tawny beige as far as the eye can see. The tablelands and the *kopjes* are behind us. Charcoal smudges, from passing puffs of clouds, stain the graded road, as we kick up a great wake of dust and gravel.

We finally reach the entrance gate to check out of the park. The squabbling starlings hope we might open a box lunch, but no such luck. We are making for Manyara. If we arrive before six we can still visit the lake.

Grant's gazelle appear in the dry grass, against a horizon of ostrich. Thomson's gazelles by the dozens soar and bound across the road. At the border of the Conservation Area we come face to face with the Masai and their cattle. We head through the woods and the oldupai, skimming past two dik-dik in the bush. We come across the same family of giraffe we had seen going in to the Olduvai Gorge. I was taking notes and had my head down. I never did understand what happened, if the large reticulated male ran across our car, leaped over us or barely missed us and went around behind, but when I lifted my head his great glossy rump was framed in the side window, like a carefully edited photograph, inches from my face. He was bucking like an outraged mustang. He might have broken the window. And I was spellbound, the camera around my neck but too paralyzed to pick it up. I dreamed about this for many weeks and still, even today, I might wake in the night and see the rump framed in the square window, the legs kicking to one side, the fury in his hooves and the wild beauty. At that instant the world stopped turning, my mind stopped turning: a freeze-frame, engraved forever on the memory.

We left the plain and started up toward the crater rim, where the moss and the lianas drip from the trees and the Masai herdsmen crowd the road with their flocks, making it hard to get by. We checked out of the area, finally, and started down the other side of the mountain, toward the cornfields and brick houses, an occasional round hut, and lilac jacaranda in bloom, against the rust red earth. These are the cultivated uplands of *Mbululand*, near the town of Karatu—where Michael, our paleontologist and guide from Olduvai was born—and reminds us how frail the balance can be, between the natural world and man's encroaching requirements.

We are over the rim into the Rift Valley, well in time for the lakes and the forest spread out below us, the water glittering under the frothy light of the fading day. Veils of fresh water, visible from the baobab-framed lookout, empty into a vast alkaline mirror, which comprises the bulk of Lake Manyara National Park.

The baboons scurry as we enter Paradise, this recovery of Eden. The dappled light, tall trees, aroma of damp freshness, embrace a scene as lush as it is lovely. Impala, giraffe and extravagant fowl inhabit this idyll. Hippos by the hundreds cluster in the pool, forming a skyline of breathless beauty. They remained here from a time when the Earth was newer. Thousands of storks, pelicans, flamingos and cormorants stretch as far as the eye can see, along the edge of the lake; they lift off the water in a mass then as if on command settle down again.

Termite mounds line our way. They are tall and red, architectural masterpieces, castles and their keeps of unsuspected magnificence. The mongoose let the ants and termites do the work, then take over and move in.

We come across the carcass of a buffalo, fresh enough to smell. Who knows how it died? Normally the lions, hyenas and vultures would have finished it off.

The air is otherwise sweet with night-blooming jasmine, and pungent with the trail of the big cats. Juicy fruits dangle from the trees and dry herbs freshen from the grass. A curtain of white butterflies blocks our trail. A vulture watches from a tree, waiting to feed if any are trampled and left behind. Fallen trunks and dead trees, like sculptures in a garden, fill the rambling streams and occasional ponds.

Little round "Sodom apples" tempt us but are inedible. The leaping impala pierce the shadows in the grove. We come upon a trampled pool. Elephant? A rickety wooden bridge, barely enough to hold the car, allows us to reach the other side. We come suddenly upon an entire herd of elephant at dusk feeding, a family of at least eight or nine: gigantic male with huge tusks, crooked and turned in on each other until they cross. Frolicking females and babies of varying ages and sizes. We watch them graze and with each step they come closer until they are only a few meters away. They are so close we can hear them chew. It is late in the day. The flash from the camera annoys the bull and his huge ears begin to flap. He considers charging, I can see it in his eyes, and he is certainly close enough to turn over the car. We keep very still.

We finally have to leave, long past park hours. On our way out we come across the rest of the elephant herd, happily yanking up great sheaths of grass and tearing leaves and bark off the trees. No one ever said feeding elephants was an orderly business. Partly for their overwhelming size and partly for their table manners the villagers hate them. Outside the park they have little chance of survival.

They are covered with fine red dust from a compliant wallow. Our own dust has accumulated after a day on the Serengeti plain. We climb the road back to the top of the basin and check into a lodge not unlike Seronera, less spectacular perhaps, with good management and courteous attention. The facilities are formula, in less than optimum working condition, but adequate for our immediate needs. We are too tired to care. The last thing I remembered was the view of the flame trees in bloom just outside the window.

SATURDAY, OCTOBER 21

Morning comes up like Homer's Aurora, "a rosy-fingered dawn". The clouds are lined with gold and are striated with dove and pearl. The gigantic flame tree outside the window, in full view now, frames the mirror-like surface of the lake below, spread out at our feet. After a hearty breakfast in the high-roofed conical dining room, and strong Tanzanian tea in the lounge, we depart, the dust still caking the inside of the van. Tomás hates dust. While he swishes a cloth over the worst of it I run back to the lodge to buy tea. A whole box of teabags costs only fifty Tanzanian shillings, at two hundred to the dollar. A postcard costs the same.

A roadblock in a nearby village stops us and Eliud is upset. "Not light enough for you to see?" asks the policeman. Eliud had unwittingly turned on his headlights. He was relieved and we could see his unwillingness to be involved, at any level, with officialdom.

We turn off at *Mto Wa Mbu,* the "Mosquito Creek" we had passed on our way through, intending to visit the market. The streets are dusty and the heat rises in waves. Trucks are pulled over on all sides, with loads of green bananas, millet, coconuts and onions. One section of the market is devoted to crafts and souvenirs and we make only a passing inspection. The things we saw were crude, obvious and expensive.

Another section is strictly cotton cloth and these stalls face the road, evidently the source of most of their trade. I was really after pictures, so headed inside to see the fruits and vegetables, then to the rear, for the grains and staples, juice and color spilling out over the stalls and across the mats on the ground.

Babies cling to their mothers' backs, wrapped, as in Mexico, in a woven shawl that frees the hands for other duties and still holds them close. The market is alive with seeds and bright eyes, with glowing bananas and satiny skin, scrawny young boys and round little girls who are curious and shy.

A tailor has installed his antique sewing machine on the board-walk and while he works he chats with the passers-by, most of them rotund women with braided heads, encased in colored cotton or sheathed in factory-made skirts, usually too tight, and t-shirts or acrylic blouses.

We return, finally, to the car and continue our journey back to Arusha. We cross a military training area, then are back on the super-highway in construction. Eliud has slowed the car down, now that he has a smooth surface. No amount of pleading or argument will convince him to go faster. Masai, carrying their spears, stride down the brand-new asphalt, leaving footprints in the gummy fresh surface. The round huts of a Masai village are an anachronism with a modern industrial installation in the background. Mount Meru looms behind the town, eighty kilometers away, and the snowy tip of Kilimanjaro is barely visible, then gone, as we round a bend.

Vivid clothes dry by the water holes. Cattle lumber through the dust, which glows rosy and gold in the light. We come upon cof-fee plantations, a Canadian wheat project, the international school, jacaranda in bloom and lush bamboo, as we approach the city. Sprawling markets, abandoned jalopies—the open hood or a lop-sided wheel—shanties, piles of grimy gunnysacks, dust in clouds and waves, bawling horns, grinding gears. The brightly colored cloth on the indolent walk of the women bringing their parcels and packages into the town—firmly balanced on the tops of their heads—seems to sway and swivel while it flows and drapes, like clothes on a line. Hips swing sideways, arms hold a spear or pole across the shoulder for the cord and the bucket at either end. Open gates to corrals and stockades reveal animals at the trough.

Checkered store-bought shirts, worn trousers, stalls with book-lets and pamphlets on China, Cuba, Islamic Asia and Africa. Trinkets for local consumption, "spare parts" everywhere, the "approved stock list", kerosene lamps, woven bags or plastic buckets, the "Chit-Chat Restaurant" and bicycles, "Tailor and Outfitters", enlargement and reduction photo-copy service, "Arusha Library", "Hairdressers and Boutique", "East Africa Booksellers, Ltd.", "Insurances", "Covi Construct, Ltd.", "Millers and Extractors", "Naaz Photo Studios", "Tawi la Clock Tower", safari companies, "clothing for the bush", curio shops and back to the "New Arusha Hotel" for lunch. When were we here? Long ago, recently? It seems familiar, it seems forever. We took refreshments at a table in the garden under the trees: bougainvillea and jacaranda, magnolia and plum. A freshly painted sign: "Do not touch the flowers". A children's swing and see-saw at the end of the grove.

Succulent Arusha, boisterous Arusha, frontier Arusha, of green lawns and tractors and insolent women with galvanized metal pails on their heads, dusty boots and hats with zippered compartments in the crown, ebony carvings and crude batik and tie-dye, ebony-colored babies, runny noses and grimy hands, crooked teeth, missing teeth, broken noses, peering eyes. A cloudless sky, a blazing sun, Mount Meru framed between the cars on a downhill street, squawk of geese and ducks, drone of flies, cool breeze, natural ease, a man on a swing—sunglasses, close-cropped black head, yellow shirt—in the hotel garden.

The Masai bazaar on the border of Namanga: hundreds of brightly dressed men, women and children in a swarm, like flies or hornets across a dry knoll, hostile except to their own.

3.

MASAI TRIBESMAN

High cheekbones, long sculptured legs, narrow shoulders, wrapped in ragged togas of tablecloth-checkered prints. A car drives up among the safari-geared foreigners. Public officials descend, in pomp and ceremony, displaying their importance. The same everywhere. Do they want something? Just passing through.

We say goodbye to Eliud. We have promised to send him a cassette of Mexican music, especially *Cielito lindo,* which he adores. When we sang it in the car he kept time not by bobbing his head up and down but by swinging his whole body from side to side, like the elephants, or the Masai or a clapper on a bell.

He eventually received it. We were pleased with the efficiency of the Tanzanian mail service, if only to his post office box. We now have a lively correspondence, and he keeps me informed of life in Arusha, with his family and on his jobs, and with his taking visitors into the parks. "But none like you," he assures me.

∫∫∫

A fat driver named George, whose belly hangs out of his A&K vest and whose front teeth are missing, picks us up on the Kenya side. We have a "puncture" on the road back toward Nairobi. While he changes the tire, or "the tyre", we amuse ourselves by walking among the thorn bushes and termite mounds, following the tracks of the Masai flocks or buffalo *spoor,* but I had learned my lesson, or so it would appear. I kept the road in full view.

We had to pull into a town called Kajiado for repairs to the inner tube. This is not a tourist town. The modest little mosque with the green trim is for the local faithful, for according to the Prophet Mohammad ("peace and blessings be upon him") green is the color of Islam, but there is no shortage of the superstitious in East Africa, because often the trim is blue, a Turkish custom, to ward off the evil eye. This has always intrigued us, we follow it to its source: When Alexander the Great invaded the Ancient Near East and Central Asia his Macedonian soldiers, many of whom remained behind to colonize and populate, had blue eyes.

4.

MOSQUE IN THE COUNTRYSIDE

We find a plethora of beauty salons, either to straighten the hair or to braid it; and the idle group of men at their afternoon chat in front of the butcher shop, to one side of the main street, is no different from Spain or Greece or Sicily. They pretend to ignore us but our presence is unsettling, they are visibly uncomfortable. We are strangers, after all.

A Masai girl, with e.e. cummings' "long, hard eyes", appeared at the petrol pump with her plastic container. She stood next to me while she had it filled. She dwarfed me with her height but she was very narrow. Her feet inside the scarred leather thong sandals were equally scarred and leathery, and very dirty. The cloth draped around her otherwise nude body was augmented by a toga, caught at one shoulder with a large safety pin. She nonchalantly reached under her left armpit for a coin purse on a cord, revealing a patch of firm, hard young skin. Her head was shaved and the proportion was small in relation to the total aesthetic, exactly the effect desired.

A walk up and down the main street revealed more of life in Kajiado: the stores where they sell, as in any small Mexican town, mattresses, cheap furniture, stoves on time payment, hardware, rope, leather harnesses. A donkey appears, carrying timber. More properly dragging the beams tied to its back with harsh hemp rope. The signs and posters fixed to the cement walls painted bright colors announce, by turns, a town meeting, a political campaign and a new awareness of religious identification.

It was late when we returned to Nairobi. Dusk was on the town and the lights were coming up, adding a certain poetry of civilization to what now seemed a sophisticated metropolis.

We were checked back into the hotel. We claimed the heavy luggage we had deposited in storage and were even given the same rooms, called suites. In effect, the living room with its television and mini-bar, desk, round dining table with chairs and overstuffed furniture, alongside a bedroom with ample closet, dressing table and full, clean bathroom in perfect working order, with potable water in the tap, all overlooking the city from the fourteenth floor, seemed not only a suite but actually a kind of grandeur we had forgotten existed. We phoned the Mexican Embassy to cancel dinner with our friends, the Ambassador and his wife, and devoted our evening to a hot shower, washing hair, rinsing out clothes and sewing on buttons. These all seemed like astonishing luxuries.

Tanzania still offers a taste of what is left of the "Green Hills" of Hemingway, but tourist-smart Kenya, in those days, was more comfort-loving and modernized, and appealed to the tourist wanting reliable plumbing, disinfected lettuce and toiletries or pharmaceutical supplies with the seal intact. Sometimes. More on this subject later.

SUNDAY, OCTOBER 22

Bound for Amboseli. Having repacked and again left suitcases in storage we are collected in the A&K van for a fifteen- or twenty-minute drive to Wilson Airport, the airfield built in the time of Beryl

Markham and Denys Finch-Hatton, on the edge of town, during our travels devoted entirely to local flights in small aircraft.

Our passage is selected from among a stack of papers and receipts we had been handed upon arrival in the country, each for a different flight. Air Kenya has a ticket counter at Wilson Airport but it will be the last we see for a long time. After check-in and admonitions regarding photography in and around the airport, a violation of military security, we are led down the tarmac and into a shed for departure proceedings, airport tax and security clearance. This all adds up to a rubber stamp on the ticket receipt.

We board a DeHavilland Twin Otter and are joined by an American pilot, who leans out the window to see if our baggage has been tossed into the bin at the rear of the plane. He reviews his controls and invites Tomás to join him in the co-pilot's seat, in the absence of the appropriate personnel. Tomás is ecstatic but also petrified. He has since taken a fancy to "miniature aviation", as he calls it, but small aircraft, coupled with claustrophobia, at that point had him tight-lipped and green.

The Muslims bound for Mombasa seem to be the only other passengers on the apron on this cloudless Sunday morning. Their aircraft is just now scuffing its way out of a hangar at the end of the field. We have the Twin Otter entirely to ourselves, for the thirty-five minute flight right back to where we had been yesterday, just to the left, that is, north, of the border at Namanga. A French family—father, mother, mother-in-law and three little boys—had been scheduled for the flight but they never appeared. "Had we known," says our pilot, "the company would have brought out a smaller plane." Tomás blanches.

The plain beneath us is barren and dusty. There is no difficulty in spotting zebra, gazelle, wildebeest, giraffe, Masai cattle, scattered huts. Kilimanjaro comes into focus in the distance, above a cluster of clouds which suddenly clears, leaving a newly-opened view: winding tracks from trucks, dry washes, the rolling knolls across the grasslands into the Rift Valley, as we bank leftward, and descend to twenty-four hundred meters.

Karen Blixen had said, "Yes, this is how it was meant to be seen, from God's eyes". Was it? I think I prefer the intimacy of ground level—it frightens the animals less—being close to the aroma of dust or damp grass, the sudden iridescence of the sun on the backs of the cattle or the sheen on the head of a Masai child—black satin, glowing and smooth—or the lace of the acacias against the sky, the silence. We are accustomed, of course, to the view from God's eyes. To the Baroness it was surely a novelty, shattering all previous impressions and assembling all over again the assumptions of the senses. A Masai village from the air seems only a series of concentric circles, not particularly interesting, stockade on the outside, huts in the inner circle. Yet as I pay closer attention I see they can be just the opposite: huts in a ring about a central stockade where the cattle are kept during the night. The whole compound is protected by a halo of thorn bushes, to keep out the lions and hyenas.

∫∫∫

We are approaching Amboseli, the game park on the Kenya side, under the shadow of the "Tall Hill", as Kilimanjaro is translated. It was once also a part of Kenya until it was ceded to Germany in a treaty that kept the mountain in Tanganyika, now Tanzania, for all time. The first account of the area is to be found in the earliest recorded observations of an engineer, Joseph John Thomson, born in Manchester of Scottish ancestry, whose name is associated with a small gazelle.

Though he was awarded the Nobel Prize in Physics in 1906 in recognition of his theoretical and practical investigation of the electron and the conduction of electricity by gases, the idea that electricity was transmitted by a charged unit related to the atom had been known, and experiments had taken place, as early as the

1830's. Yet despite Thomson's invaluable contribution, his greatest pleasure was his recognition as the first European to set foot in Masai country and live to tell his story.

In 1882 he entered what was then known as the Njiri Plains from Loitokitok, the swampland and water holes of the original Masai clans, accompanying a Swahil slave-hunter, Juma Kimemata, on his way from the coast overland to Lake Victoria, by that time identified by John Hanning Speke for London's Royal Geographical Society. Juma hoped to buy his way through to Uganda, where slaves were easily obtained, using among other enticements—cloth, wire, tools, weapons—the highly prized trading beads—those cylindrical bits of Murano glass so favored among the tribes of Africa—for safe passage through the shortest possible route, then back with his ivory and human cargo to the slave markets of Zanzibar. By today's standards such practices are loathsome, but nineteenth century economies, despite public opinion to the contrary, ran on the wealth, repugnant or not, hypocritical or not, generated by colonization, yet even before, from the immemorial trade of the caravans across Central Asia, fortunes were made and lost in commerce, and the most valued products on the one hand were the best paid on the other. Nothing has changed. *Homo sapiens* still has a lot to learn, but then evolution, as we saw in Odulvai, is very slow.

Thomson made careful records of life in the Kilimanjaro region and described the animals with care and concern, yet was among the most jubilant of hunters, both for sport and "for the pot". He also made note of the vast numbers of the herds of zebra, wildebeest, hartebeest, eland and gazelle, that roamed the plains of Amboseli, accompanied by their predators, the lion, cheetah and leopard, packs of hyena and the equally vicious wild dog. He actually managed to leave head counts of the great number of black rhino but surprisingly, he found few buffalo or elephant, which were later introduced into the region, to the detriment of the ecological balance in the area of the Ol Tukai water hole. The error was compounded in the division of the district into two separate regions, to the consternation of the territorial animals whose parameters were thus limited, to Amboseli in the south, with the northern extension encompassed within Nairobi National Park on the outskirts of a burgeoning capital and its suburbs.

Green woodland, scrub growth, waterholes, herds of elephant, have now appeared under the shadow of the great mountain lurking to our right. We are on the ground, a perfect landing. No one comes around to meet us but we haul our gear aboard a Land Rover bound for the lodge. What could be simpler? Once installed we find a pleasant compound across the rough lawn, facing the mountain, with swimming pool, cabins whose water is heated by solar units and mosquito netting over the beds. Floor is clay tile, furniture is pine that has been sanded and varnished. It is very hot. We leave our bags and head for the main building, with its wide veranda of leather and slat chairs. Tea is served all day in the lounge. The merchandise in the shop is supplied by Nairobi's "African Heritage", enough to attract Tomás, the inveterate shopper, until we are startled to see, through the slats of the chair, a solitary Masai in disdainful splendor seated at the bar, his sandaled feet hitched through the crosspiece of the barstool, his spear at his side. He observes the hotel employees and the occasional guest passing through with undisguised curiosity, while they stare back in awe, perhaps a little fear, definitely amazement, and give him a wide berth.

We run into Alan, our first driver, whom we greet as an old friend. He is the only familiar face around. We tell him we were never met and have no idea with whom to make our game drives. He immediately solves everything, arranges for a car and driver and sends us off before the day gets any hotter.

The plain is wide and very open, with abundant wildebeest, zebra, some gazelle; and then a herd of elephant crosses our path, to our bewildered delight. Both cows and bulls are more concerned for the calves in the family than with the invasion of outsiders and they ignore us, stopping only to urinate right in front of the car. This is apparently a standard gesture. "They are leaving messages," says Tomás. "Just as dogs do. It's their way of reading the daily newspaper. How many females around? Are they in heat? What cologne are the males wearing? Everyday stuff."

We see a few rhino at a distance, in the swamp grass, then giraffe in an acacia grove and a pack of rollicking, disrespectful baboon. The males stride right up to the car and stare us straight in the eye. Their walk is jerky and arrogant. The hind quarters, slim and spare, move like a dog's. The forequarters, being higher, with the arms much longer than the legs, move at a different pace and rhythm, making one baboon seem like two different creatures under the same hide. The head is held very stiffly and the look is suspicious and haughty, the golden eyes flashing fire and self-righteousness. They look like nothing so much as government magistrates, throwing their weight around.

The females, meantime, remain in the background, carrying the smallest of the babies, that cling to their breast and ride upside down, or larger youngsters who ride on mama's back as if she were some sort of horse. Mama, in fact, might be pulling along a third child by the hand, like a harassed housewife in a neighborhood supermarket.

The sky is closing in around Kilimanjaro, framed in clouds which seem suspended, as if in a Magritte painting. It is nearly dusk, with vivid clarity and a singing dark and dryness. Kilimanjaro has snow on its southern rather than its northern slope. We are south of the Equator. The constellations are reversed, even the water spinning down a drain or wash basin is reversed. The Milky Way, a murky film, is a gauze, a veil, thrown across the starry night. In reverse.

MONDAY, OCTOBER 23

The night is warm, an invitation to rise early, disentangling ourselves from the dusty mosquito netting, which is full of holes. The rooms in the hotel are large enough but there is no place to put anything and this takes getting used to. Our things are at first strewn about the floor.

A square hole in the window is filled with mesh to keep out monkeys and mosquitoes, but the pane opens inward, curtailing the possibility of using the surface of the desk or dressing table just under it for items of any consequence; the monkeys will simply reach in and take them. This makes for good housekeeping, since the room is entered, as well, by a stable door and while this looks charming it is impractical. Even with the window closed we soon have monkeys inside the room, inspecting our luggage. The pillow is a foam-rubber tablet, which they are not averse to nibbling. And heaven help us if we leave our pencils and notebooks unattended.

The dawn, however, is clear, vibrant with birds and insects; and the monkeys are shrewd and observant. They play in the trees, dash across the garden and make the best use of the breakfast fruit that other guests have left on the tables. They are grayish with blue-tipped hair, like feathers, that clings neatly to their firm, hard little bodies. A large scarlet disc outlines the male's anus, the testicles are bright turquoise and the penis is cherry red. Nature went mad.

We take coffee in the lounge, then go out on an early morning's game drive before breakfast. The people in the cars around us are dwelling on the "shock" and the "revolting spectacle" of a dawn kill, as if it were vicious and mean, but there is nothing genocidal or cruel about it, and the animals have no political agenda or hidden meaning, nor even the cruelty of a slaughter-house. They are simply keeping their numbers in balance and food on the table.

There was a time when outsiders encroached on Africa with the mounting of great expeditions. They brought utensils, medicines, weapons and ammunition, scientific instruments, writing materials, furnishings for their campsite, bathtub and personal gear, and to carry it all hired bearers, who often robbed and abandoned them or who succumbed to unfamiliar diseases as they traveled from one region to another, or who fell afoul of the rampant slave trade.

And these European outsiders learned, at great cost, how to conserve and disinfect their water supply and they wisely brought their own food since only the natives—who were generally hostile to outsiders— can live off the land, know which plants, insects or animals can be eaten, how to gather and prepare them, and it was all very complicated, often for little reward.

Now Africa is accessible. All one needs is a camera, walking shoes and a good hat. Oh, yes, and the necessary inoculations. There were no vaccines or antibiotics in the nineteenth or early twentieth centuries, and there were further dangers from the mutual antagonism of a diversity of European intruders. So who disrupted the balance? A lioness out hunting for her breakfast or the White Hunters with high powered rifles and heavy ammunition? Or the ivory traders, who often transported tons at a time? Or perhaps the explorers, opening the continent to the ravages of alien customs and concerns?

We are only, at this moment, a few meters from the sight of a wandering family of elephant, two sleeping cheetahs, a picked-over zebra carcass and a vast panorama of dead or dying trees. Many blame the elephants and their sloppy eating habits, others the caprice of the water supply, but it is mostly people like ourselves who intrude on Amboseli's fragile ecology and the alkaline surface is ground to a powder, then stirred by the moving vehicles, that carry the very customers who pay to maintain the park and to keep the animals alive. We are killing the entire area and accelerating the process of encroaching desert that will eventually force Amboseli to be abandoned, to let Nature find her own way. This is a daunted, even a dismayed Paradise, under the baleful gaze of marauding vultures, the *end* of Eden.

After a staggering buffet lunch—twenty-six different kinds of salad, chicken curry, rice, stew, excellent Kenyan cheeses and at least a dozen desserts—I went out to walk three times around the garden, virtually the only exercise available outside of a swim. A massive invasion of German and American tourists found me more than a little amusing, by this time covered with dust and intent on my notebook. They were ornithologists on an African field trip, busy with their own binoculars and notebooks, checking off what they had seen against the list of available species.

A game drive took us into a fetid swamp, that seemed painted or blotched in abstract, half mud, half dust. There were abundant but indifferent buffalo, elephant, hippo, wildebeest and zebra, graceful egret, honking geese and flirting kori bustard. A dead wildebeest had been invaded by vultures to finish off Nature's carefully ordered hierarchy of a time-shared food supply, to be followed only by a succession of insects until nothing is left, or so we thought.

Nearby a pair of hyenas frolicked in a pond. They suddenly abandon their gambol. One of them bounds off like a badly assembled bicycle in the dust while the other moves, strangely alert and graceful, despite the heavy forequarters and square head, to disband the vultures by its simple presence. It tears at the carcass, then turns over the whole body in a simple, single jerk and yank. There is still an ample meal on the underside so the food supply cycle begins all over again.

A whole train of elephant is playing and feeding while it approaches the swamp in front of us, filing down toward the cool green from the dusty knoll, uprooting grass as it ambles along, both with the trunk and with the toes, that tap tentatively at anything that grows, until it is gleefully and maliciously caught in a firm grip. One huge male seems arrested during a dust bath. He is twisted and stranded—crippled or somehow distorted—while trying to lumber to his feet. We watch carefully, wondering whether or not to report his predicament, but then he manages to rise laboriously, grunting at us and staring, before he plods off in the dust and the setting sun to rejoin his family.

A rhino appears on a hedged crest between the watery plain and the dry knoll. He is an armored locomotive, an anachronism, a sympathetic monster: powerful mass, clumsy fool. Whoever said his horn was aphrodisiac? And if it is not, what good is he? What place have the animals in a world too crowded and too bent on industrialization to keep them alive? The mesh of Nature is so fine; we will never fully detect the keenness of her order, until it is much too late.

The absurd frogs are in full chorus, calling to the dazzling sky. A roaring driftwood fire warms the lounge. The tea is strong and black. *"There is no fat on this land,"* Karen Blixen said, *"no luxuriance anywhere."* The geographical position and the altitude *"combined to create a landscape that had not its like in all the world."*

TUESDAY, OCTOBER 24

The waiter in the lounge last night said he hated the food in the hotel. Kenyan people are strong and healthy, he says, because they eat maize and beans, mashed together and fried; and also because they work hard and lift heavy things, "much building".

We finish our fruit and depart for the landing strip. Our schedule originally indicated that we would return to Wilson Airport in Nairobi to make the connection to Nyeri but since there were no other passengers the Kenyan captain and the Afro-Indian co-pilot simply guided the Twin-Otter directly into the Aberdare Mountains for the fifty-five minute flight. As we take off above the egrets, the vultures and the hawk-eagles soaring over the swamp, their wingtips gleaming in the morning light, the desert stretches into the distance and Kilimanjaro, a wide, sloping silhouette, is embraced by a few wafts of cotton candy and taffy clouds.

The landscape changes to farm country, laid out in perfect squares around a winding river. These rolling hills, the tea plantations, lumber mills, the horse and dairy farms, were the background for a whole generation of British émigrés, who raised their children in a temperate climate, not unlike that of England itself, but wild and free, in a strange union with the animals in the bush and the birds in the sky. Even the dogs were different. Beryl Markham's once killed a leopard.

The flight was perfect and the landing flawless. We are met by a battered bus and an amiable driver named Joseph. The door swings on broken hinges. The windows rattle. The poor, old bus climbs, with great effort, up a graded road lined with gum trees, through fruit groves and grazing land. The thorny acacias of Amboseli have given way to pines and eucalyptus. The rocky road is dusty and sisal marks the fence lines, before open grain fields and the sheep and goats at their pasture. A number of the farm houses are made of logs, with metal roofs, others are batten and board and still others are luxurious dwellings of stone with heavy beams and broad driveways. The corrals and sheds enclose fine Holstein dairy cattle and trim-looking, well-bred horses.

Aberdare Country Club, our destination, is named for the baronet granted in 1873 to Henry Austin Bruce of Duffryn in the Welsh county of Glamorgan. In 1882 he began an association with West Africa that lasted the rest of his life, by accepting the chairmanship of the National African Company formed by Sir George Goldie, which in 1886 received a charter under the title *Royal Niger Company*, antecedent of the founding of the protectorate of Nigeria. In gratitude Lord Aberdare was knighted in 1885, and in appreciation he established the charters that would eventually become the University of Wales, now Cardiff University. His descendants have been allowed to remain among the ninety-two elected hereditary peers, according to the House of Lords Act of 1999, and remain in Parliament to this day.

The manager of the club, who comes out to greet us, is gracious and accommodating; we are politely told to wait until time for departure to a game-viewing site called "The Ark", so while Tomás looks over the work of a guild of independent artisans I go exploring.

The guest rooms are actually small houses, much more solid and substantial, and certainly more charming, than the term "bungalow" or "cottage" would imply. Each is separate from the others and built of stone with a large living room, fireplace, and a dining table that divides two bedroom areas, one with king size and the other with twin beds, each of these with a very luxurious and sizable bathroom, closets and storage space for gear that would reasonably complement the Club's facilities: golf, tennis, swimming, riding, hunting, game viewing or simple vacationing, with jogging trails, bridge tables, reading room, art supplies, or any one of many pursuits deemed genteel and respectable to a population still governed by British standards. My enthusiasm, however, was wasted, though I had yet to learn that none of this was to be ours.

There is also ornithology facilitated by an aviary on the grounds, in themselves a park, in fact, a botanical garden, informal but complete with flowering plants and trees, shrubbery and woods that finally blend, beyond the stables, into the natural setting of a private game park.

It was here, striding along a road that led past the maintenance and supply quarters and bound for the stables to pet the horses that I ran into a subdued and well-behaved but gleeful trio of young boys, about eight or ten years old. Two were brothers, Simon and Frederick. The other, smaller, was a school chum of Simon's on holiday. The families all live in Nairobi and are guests of the Club, of which they are members.

The children were eager to get acquainted with a stranger from such a far-off place as Mexico, and were surely among the few people in Africa to know where Mexico was or to have any notion of its place in Western affairs. They dragged me off to see the one-and-one-half month old orphaned eland, being fed from a bottle but not likely, says the attending zoologist, to survive.

Simon then took me down to the corral, to fondle the horses that wandered over to see if we had any sugar, with names like "Super-Charger", "Night King Call" and "Betty". Simon was very keen on learning how to break and train a horse, how to ride, and what a proper horse should eat. He was sitting astride the wooden cross-bars of the corral fence while I leaned against it, offering a smattering of equine expertise, when a car came along, with Simon and Frederick's mother Margaret at the wheel, and a passenger, Reena, sent out from Ireland, who was working in Kenya with the Catholic Mission.

They invited me to join them for a spin through the game park but mostly we talked. Here were two first-hand interviews, one with an Englishwoman, wife of a hydraulic engineer who has lived fifteen years in East Africa, had her children and sent them to school here, run a house and kept servants, done charity work, taken holidays and attended company parties; and yet still talks about "going home" to England.

The other was an idealist when she came out, a devout Catholic, dealing with problems of birth control, infant mortality, induced abortion, premature death, labor pains without antisepsis or antibiotics and vaccination campaigns, but mostly AIDS and the endemic transmission of the HIV virus, whose origin—to this day a mystery—had been arbitrarily assigned by the rest of the world to Africa and Africans. Those infected by the transfusion of contaminated blood were somehow perceived as "innocent victims" of a rampaging disease, then reaching plague proportions, spreading to ten times more men than women, for which homosexual men and heroin addicts were perceived as the most "guilty" of all, in no way "victims". This was 1989, and as Dr. Abraham Verghese later pointed out in his book, **My Own Country, a Doctor's Story** (New York, Simon & Schuster, 1994,

p. 251), *"...the virus, unlike human beings, lacked all class prejudice. The proof of this was Africa, where HIV behaved like gonorrhea or syphilis: men and women were affected in equal numbers. In Africa, other sexually transmitted diseases which cause open ulcers on the genitals were common and deemed to thereby facilitate the transmission of HIV. Another widely touted reason for the democratic spread of the virus in Africa was that friable scar tissue from female circumcision made vaginal intercourse somewhat traumatic, prone to cause microscopic bleeding, made it akin to anal intercourse. Since these "facts" about HIV in Africa were standard fare in any [Western] journalist's update on AIDS, it had become possible for middle America to believe—if only subconsciously—that since Africans practiced female circumcision, copulated indiscriminately and suffered chronically from other sexually transmitted infections, they too were in some way "guilty..."*

Question: What is the principal cause of AIDS in East Africa?

Answer: Promiscuity. "The lorry drivers," Reena explains, "come up from Mombasa, full of it, and after they hit the shantytown in Nairobi, the horrible Kibera, it spreads like wildfire."

Question: What makes Kibera different from any other shantytown slum?

Answer: "I don't recommend your looking in to find out, but if you do, don't go alone. It is famous for rampant prostitution, the only way women have of getting along, as the men refuse, or are too drunk or drugged, to work. About the only effort they make is illicit. Drugs, arms dealing, trafficking in humans, so as you can see, the slave trade is far from dead. They make illegal whiskey from hidden stills. It's dreadful and often poisonous. There is a lot of unemployment and despair, a vicious circle; and vice, overcrowding and murder. Endemic alcoholism. None of these is a new problem and there is certainly nothing original here, but the extent is tremendous and the possibility for a remedy is nil.

Question: Why aren't more of these people back in their villages or with their tribes, growing food?

Answer: "A man cannot be buried except on his own land and there is none left to distribute. This affects inheritance laws and gives them a political as well as a sociological overtone. Meantime, the climate of demoralization grows and grows."

We talked about independence and its diverted hopes, about the failed East African Federation, elephants astray on the Tsavo highway—every day growing more scarce when once their numbers amounted literally to millions, and no one knows what to do with them. We talked about poaching, women's rights and the problems of keeping house in the middle of Africa, while the boys listened, or hung out the car window, trying to pet a passing giraffe or catch a closer look at the stately antelope called the eland, perhaps the abandoned calf's parents. Here we could park anywhere at will, walk about at will, take a wrong turn and double back at will. There was no registration, no ranger at the gate, no warning against serpents or leopards. "Are you mad?" laughs Reena. "The leopard is nearly extinct."

We finally returned to refreshments on the lawn, a courtesy of the Club, while we rejoined our respective friends. Tomás might have been bewildered at my long absence but he knew when he saw my face that it was surely productive. Simon and Frederick and Margaret their mother, their father and an uncle, together with Reena, after waving our farewells, had moved toward the oak-paneled dining room for a cruise-type buffet luncheon, lavish and abundant, with the ever-present salads and local cheeses, top grade meat and poultry, hard-boiled eggs and a diversity of vegetables, as well as an astonishing variety of desserts.

Another ride, this time on a better bus, within the Club precinct, to a sturdy and sizable wooden construction facing the Yasabara Water Hole. A cross between a hotel and a cruise ship, The Ark, faithful to its name, presupposes one hundred people who enter two by two to settle in, with only a small handbag each, to tiny staterooms: two bunks, a night table between them, a curtained window overlooking the woods falling away on all sides, blankets for the cold night, coat hooks. The bathroom, in the fashion of a dormitory or a luxury campsite, is communal, one for men, one for women, at the end of the hall, but of fine quality and with all the amenities.

A lounge provides tea, coffee and cookies (biscuits) through the night. The dining room, entered in response to a bell, supplies supper that night and breakfast the next morning, at long tables for eight each, in the greatest economy of space. And I thought we would be staying in one of the elegant stone "cottages"!!

Different open-air terraces or enclosed observation decks, with admonitions to keep the voice down, permit direct viewing of the animals, from early evening through the entire night and into the early morning, as the beasts presume to come down to the salt lick and water hole. We are in the center of 767 square kilometers of Aberdare National Park, at just over 1800 meters above sea level, the facility constituted in 1950 and situated between two peaks: *Kinangop* (3905 meters) and *Oldonyo Lesatimma* (3999 meters). The view is like nothing so much as a painting by Cuban artist Tomás Sánchez, with dense vegetation closing in on a pool of water, hyper-realism, yes, but breathy, damp and cool. For a closer look there is a "hide", with peepholes for photography, no flash, please, reached at the basement level of the structure. A carpet of large, sharp stones all around the basement guarantees that even the most curious animals will keep their distance.

We therefore descended from the bus, stood in line in order to proceed and then minced in orderly and obedient fashion across the wooden catwalk into The Ark, feeling a bit like the flight crews in *Moonraker,* or the menagerie assembled by John Huston for his role as Noah in *The Bible.*

High-powered reflectors, intended to simulate moonlight, are guaranteed to keep the animals amused without offending them, or so we are told, thus becoming the most blatant moonlight of all. As long as noise is kept to a minimum, says our private Noah in the long beard and tunic—the manager of The Ark who stands at the entrance to see us inside—none of them seems to mind.

The buffalo did breathe a little harder for awhile and the lions did keep their distance, only announcing their presence with their grunting before dawn. As night fell, however, we had more mosquitoes than any other species of wildlife, and then a drenching tropical rain announced the onset of the monsoon season. A miraculous display of insect wings was revealed before our incredulous eyes, caught in the light from the reflectors, but the downpour managed to discourage almost everything else. The Ark is for people, after all, who are on the inside looking out and who probably represent, according to Tomás, the specie in the greatest danger of extinction. The animals on the outside are free to come and go at will unless, as I came to suspect, they are herded up here to satisfy our appetite for rarefied game viewing.

The spirals and flutters of demented light from the insects in the rain finally subsided. A lone heron crossed the ground below, a serval cat, a Cape hare, then a small band of hardy buffalo appeared, along a path they had chosen as surely the safest. They preceded to the salt lick, in hierarchical order, first the leader and then the others. A buffalo of a different breed also materialized out of the shadows but from another direction. He was no doubt a solitary male, a renegade from the bachelor's club, that phenomenon that retires the aged no longer fit for an active life or the otherwise unworthy, that have survived the lions' pruning of the herd. He had to ask an "alpha male", that is, the herd's leader, for permission to remain; and waited his turn for the salt.

Carnivores, as might be assumed, have no need for salt. If they come here at all it is to find the herbivores, like these buffalo, that really need less of the salt provided by the hotel than they eat; but like junk-food addicted children they enjoy the treat. They even urinate a good distance away, to avoid contaminating their toy.

As I study them from the "hide", the artificial moon gleams on their silk and velvet muzzles, the horns polished on acacia shrubs, the moisture of the tongue and the soft eyes that turn fierce in an instant, as I recall from my "incident" in Seronera. I can hear their breathing, the stamping of their hooves, the rubbing of hair as one rump brushes against another, like commuters on a crowded urban train.

The fireflies are out and an occasional falling star. A male bushbuck halts to sniff the wind. He knows the lion is near and he is skittish. Soon his mate peers from the low, raindrop-tipped branches and the drops scatter, in slow motion, under the steady light from the undaunted reflectors. A large hyena scurries by and then disappears. The heron returns, to feed by the edge of the water. The herd of buffalo actually starts to settle down for the night but the rumbling lion drives them off, down the same path by which they arrived. The lone male also leaves, by his own path, on the opposite side of the water hole.

WEDNESDAY, OCTOBER 25

Later, after about three hours of sleep, I jump from my bunk, certain I must have missed something. A special alarm system, if left turned on, will rouse the drowsing guest from his slumber, in case something special or wonderful really does start to happen. This was not the case. It was by my own private alarm and it was three in the morning. I slipped my fatigue-green padded vest over my rumpled shirt and went to wash my face, then tried the lounge to see what was going on. A guide—the kind of man who would once have been considered a "white hunter" but who in today's world is no more than a baby-sitter for a luxury group of tourists—was trying to romance one of the women in his party. The huge fire in the fireplace was dying down and the windows were steamy. The water for the tea was not hot enough. The cookies were gone and had not been replaced. A single steward dozed near the bar.

There were no more than half a dozen people intent on what might happen and, in fact, nothing did. Another Cape hare came into view. A mongoose, accompanied by a bushbuck, nuzzled a little water. Ducks and geese began to appear as dawn approached. The windows and ledges were covered with a layer of fluff: the residue from the moths and mosquitoes that had died in the rain or in the light from the reflectors. Fog and low clouds closed in, obliterating shapes and turning the ferns on the high hills into vague colors, strange sizes, indefinable varieties of sound that moved in the sheltered pockets of giant heather and rosewood, the icy trout streams and cascades that fell into the bamboo forest below.

After breakfast we were assembled on the deck, Noah bid us farewell with an indifferent wave of his hand, and then the bus took us down through the monkey-branched woods, back to the Aberdare Country Club. We collected our baggage, the parcels from the shop and were deposited without further ceremony on the airstrip to await our Cessna 402, for the fifteen minute flight eastward to Nanyuki, only four hundred meters higher than Nyeri, close to the slopes of Mt. Kenya. Our pilot is a Hindu Indian, his co-pilot Sikh, his head enveloped in a pious white turban. They collect the piece of paper that corresponds to a ticket and stash our bags in the hold. We fly over rich farm and grazing land, native villages and ostentatious homes with the impressive chimneys of many fireplaces; and then we land.

The landing strip is paved. It lies in an area among huts and flocks of sheep inside languid, rolling hills, soft woodland and a broad plateau. The landscape beyond sweeps northward, where we creep along a highway in construction, through cloying, thick mud and scattered rocks, to a collection of wooden shacks with souvenirs and a large sign announcing that we are right on the Equator. Did we know bodies weigh one percent less at the Equator? We stop for a photograph. We step over the line. We are now back in the Northern Hemisphere. Another step. Southern Hemisphere.

Another step... After awhile we tire of the game and in any case it begins to rain.

We have now reached the well-advertised and quite opulent Mt. Kenya Game Park and Safari Club, established in 1959 by the late William Holden at the very height of his prodigious and prolific acting career and, after his untimely death, partially supported by his erstwhile companion, actress Stephanie Powers. For twenty-five years the now-departed film star and Don Hunt, among his Kenyan partners, collected animals from the area around *Kirinyaga,* the sacred mountain of the Kikuyu tribe—known as Mount Kenya, 5199 meters high—mostly orphans that had been endangered by excessive hunting or encroaching farms and towns, and relocated them in the game park, to be protected as part of Kenya's heritage, or if such were the case, transferred to zoos or other game parks around the world.

The Club was originally a hideaway for a select group of friends, so they could drink, swap stories and headquarter their safaris, but it grew into an institution and world-renowned five-star hotel, with golf course, riding stables, tennis courts, lawn bowling, swimming pool; and over the years a roster of nobility and celebrity among the guests.

The magnificent grounds include a remarkable selection of rare storks, Egyptian geese, ibis, cranes of several varieties, and both the all-white and blue eyed (not albino) snowy peacock, and the better known iridescent blue-and-green Christus Palawan phaisan, or Persian peacock. All wander at will across the gardens and among the cottages, followed by the swarms of monkeys that scurry out of the forest.

The Mt. Kenya Safari Club is more demanding, with stricter rules, than the more informal Aberdare Country Club, more calculated for the effect of its peculiar chic. The main building encloses a central patio and fountain and includes very expensive shops, a delightful lounge overlooking the gardens and the mountains beyond, and tea every afternoon, enveloped in a décor which includes the ample use of zebra skins, oriental rugs, handsome tusks and an important collection of African art, especially Nigerian bronzes. Women must wear a dress and men a jacket and tie after five in the afternoon. Food is excellent and service well-trained and discreet, though one waiter, jubilant to learn we were from Mexico, asked in an uncharacteristic outburst if soccer star Hugo Sánchez was a personal friend.

We are roughly at the altitude of Mexico City, about 2400 meters. Lunch consists in a posh buffet and as we look over our salads we are startled by a parade of waiters singing "Happy birthday to you" in Swahili, while they hold aloft a proud but tiny birthday cake, the candles lit. "*Si kukuni yako, si kukuni yako...*"

"*This is your day, your very great day*". We start to laugh and I follow the little parade to a nearby table. "Someone here is a Scorpio," I announce, by way of introduction. "And so am I." The lady being honored is from England and is traveling with her husband, her son and one daughter. They have come to Kenya to meet two other daughters in their early twenties who are now at the half-way point in a trip around the world. We chatted for a moment, declined the offer to join them but saw them a number of times after that—they were staying at a private home in the forest nearby—and exchanged addresses in case our paths should ever again cross. My new Scorpio friend, Veronica, offered well-taken advice to be applied the following week when we reached the coast, but more of that in good time.

THURSDAY, OCTOBER 26

After a walloping buffet breakfast—fresh pineapple, papaya, cantaloupe and watermelon, followed by juices, omelettes prepared to order, Canadian bacon, Spanish *jabugo* cured ham, German sausages, Dutch canned ham, kippers, roast potatoes, chilli if we ask for it, yoghurt with fresh berries, spiced prunes, home-made croissants, *pain au chocolat* and *brioche*, and gallons of Kenyan tea and coffee with fresh milk and clotted cream— we finally waddle across the central courtyard, tentatively testing the air for the inevitable drizzle of the season.

The peacocks are intent on their courtship rites, the males fluttering the extended fan of their immense tail feathers like divas at the opera, the females indifferent and bored. Macaws and cockatoos call from the aviary. Tomás is in the shops, mentally fashioning new jewelry designs while he examines the East African gem stones, especially the rich violet, nearly black, Tanzanite, a rather new find at that time.

Africa's anomalies are commonplace today but during the European land grab of the nineteenth century the notion of snow-covered peaks year-round on the Equator was still bewildering, especially in view of Herodotus, much earlier, publishing his commentary on the mystery of Egypt's Nile. The persistent historian of Asia Minor (c. 484-425 B.C., born in Halicarnassus, Caria, today's Bodrum on the Turkish coast), the father not of history, as Cicero later dubbed him, but rather of journalism and reportage—he could weave a great yarn—asked how this vast quantity of water and fertile silt could cross nearly four thousand kilometers of burning desert, to nourish the Mediterranean coastline, and never fail from one season to the next.

Perhaps Ptolemy was right, mused the later geographers, when he claimed, c. 150 B.C., in his remarkable world map, that the water resulted from the snow melt of the Ruwenzori, which he called the "Mountains of the Moon", poised on the Rift in Central Equatorial Africa. But how could this be? How could the water maintain its thrust and volume, and flow north, yes north, over mountains, valleys and deserts, for a total of some eight thousand kilometers?

Gaius Plinius Secundus, Roman author, naturalist and philosopher known as "Pliny the Elder", was born in Como in A.D. 25 and died during the eruption of Vesuvius at Pompeii in A.D. 79, but among his works we have the *Naturalis Historia,* one of the largest single works to have survived Imperial Rome, covering the entire field of ancient knowledge, especially as concerns botany, zoology, art, astronomy, geology, mineralogy and inventions of the time since confirmed by archaeological investigation. He was, like everyone else, concerned with the source of the Nile—whoever controlled the Nile controlled Africa— and served as a reference during Napoleon Bonaparte's African campaign of 1799.

Herodotus, Ptolemy and Pliny, like the long list of daring and inquisitive men who came after them, not only asked the same question. They sought the answer by the logical strategy of following the great river along its bank or by navigating its green depths, all without success. Even if they managed to survive the cataracts, terrible heat, hippos and crocodiles, they would be defeated by the endless desert, insects and disease, and then come to a halt at the Sudd, the vast and fetid swampland, virtually impossible to cross, source of fevers that as yet had no name.

Richard Francis Burton (1821-1890), an English geographer, explorer, translator, prolific author, captain in the British army, controversial Orientalist, cartographer, ethnologist, poet, diplomat, expert swordsman, a linguist who spoke at least twenty-nine languages and a spy, famous for his exploits in Arabia when newly circumcised and disguised as a local merchant he entered Mecca on pilgrimage and circled the Kabah, undetected, and survived to tell the story, decided the inland route was the wiser choice, and headed west from Zanzibar. His adventures were many, he almost died, and his observations carefully detailed the land and its people. In effect, he reached the Mountains of the Moon, and he also laid eyes on a great lake, but then took ill and was unable to accompany his ambitious, but careless, second in command, John Hanning Speke (1827-1864), who left the ailing Burton in camp and made his way with a contingent of bearers, saw a larger lake that he named Victoria, but without reconnaissance or verification proclaimed it, on the basis of intuition alone, to be the source of the Nile. Burton objected. He visualized a chain of interconnected lakes, and so it would be, but not the one he had seen.

It was Sir Samuel White Baker (1821-1893), explorer, big game hunter, engineer, writer and abolitionist, holder of the titles of Pasha and Major-General in the Egypt of the Ottoman Empire, in fact the Governor General of the Equatorial Nile Basin—the colony of Equatoria— who designed a collapsible boat that could be removed from the swamp and ferried around to the next stretch of river. He was accompanied by his second wife, Florence, hardy and resourceful and an excellent shot, his first wife Henrietta having died in 1855. After overcoming incredible obstacles he and Florence finally outwitted the wily Sudd and discovered the lake Baker named Albert, a link in the White Nile chain, which verified Speke's discovery of Lake Victoria but also ratified Burton's clever estimation of an inter-related lake system.

This left only the matter of the river's thrust, which had been solved much earlier, though no one believed him, by Scotland's James Bruce (1730-1794), an intrepid explorer who in the course of his travels in Ethiopia traversed a series of steep and narrow canyons (which acted as chutes) to reach the headstream of the Blue Nile at Lake Tana, at the time presumed to be the Nile's main source. He reported his findings in *Travels to Discover the Source of the Nile* (1790). Future cartography would verify the thrust of the Blue Nile, which joins the great volume of water in the White Nile at Khartoum to form a single durable and hearty stream, capable of forging its way across the desert to Egypt. Bruce's recounting of "the steak carved from the living cow" caused more furor than his explorations of the river, as he described the customs of the thrifty tribes in the interior, who instead of slaughtering an animal for their food simply hacked out a chunk of rump, which would later heal, to be eaten again. The outrage was so great his findings were discounted.

Though Burton's Central African explorations would be, for a time, discredited he did come upon long, slender Lake Tanganyika, at its head or northern end a part of the basin of the Congo River and at its foot, to the south, as Scottish missionary David Livingstone would discover, the source of the River Zambezi. And on behalf of Livingstone the greatest of all the African explorers would enter the scene, an illegitimate Welsh outcast, product of a local prostitute and the town drunk. They named him John Rowlands, like his father, and he was abandoned by his parents to an orphanage from which he finally at age thirteen escaped, finding passage aboard a coal ship bound for New Orleans, where he would meet his mentor and take the name of Henry M. Stanley. He chose "Morton" for the "M".

But Stanley's lifelong inventiveness, his outrageous audacity, his cunning and cruelty, were just at the gestation period. He stole his sponsor's property, ran off to join the Confederate Army in the American Civil War, was imprisoned, escaped, and found work as a reporter. His greatest story was his meeting with James Gordon Bennett, owner of the New York Herald. He sold him the idea for the journalistic coup of the century, a quest to find and rescue Britain's hero, missionary and explorer David Livingstone.

Bennett sent Stanley (1841-1904) after ten prior stories, and his intrepid reporter found and filed them all. Stanley afterward rescued Emir Pasha of Equatoria and was hired by King Leopold of Belgium to explore the basin and to map the course of the Congo River. He was ruthless and single-minded; his iron will withstood heat and disease, bad water, tribal disputes, mutiny among his officers, abandonment by his bearers. He tracked and in effect ferreted out the elusive Scottish missionary and explained that the British press and officialdom was keen to have abolitionist Livingstone back in the United Kingdom but he refused to go.

By that time Livingstone, gravely ill, had crossed the continent from coast to coast, the only man ever to have done so, and he was frail and ailing when Stanley finally tracked him to Ujiji, on the shores of "his" Lake Tanganyika. They met, "I presume", on November 10, 1871; why the stiff and reticent presentation? They were in the middle of Africa, it could be no other. But Livingstone was Stanley's idol, and also his ticket to immortality. The medical doctor, missionary, healer, explorer, the indefatigable and monumental David Livingstone, left Henry Morton Stanley nearly speechless with awe.

Livingstone never went back to Europe. Stanley was left with his notebooks and diaries to prove they had met and they traveled together extensively, shared illness, hunger, exhaustion and privation, in fact Livingstone became the kind and approving father Stanley, in his childhood, had never known, and Livingstone, furthermore, was the only person Stanley never deceived or betrayed.

And it was Stanley who finally assembled the pieces in the jigsaw puzzle of the source of the Nile yet technically, even today, the true source remains unknown. Is it the small stream known as the Kagera, that rises in the remotest canyons of the highest peaks of the Mountains of the Moon? Which of those incipient trickles of snow melt in a hidden stream, deep in the Ruwenzori, sends the first drop of water down to Lake Victoria, to begin the strange and elusive odyssey of the Emperor of all Rivers?

We decide to visit the Animal Orphanage, one of the prime attractions of Mt. Kenya Game Park. A ten dollar admission contributes to the upkeep and well worth it, I must say. A vast and varied little family: *duiker* (pronounced "die-care"), a chimpanzee and a hyrax. A bush pig, actually a larger and stockier version of the wart hog. The strange and withdrawn civet cat, spotted body, long striped tail, which if ingested by humans presumably causes respiratory ailments, such as the SAARS epidemic in China in 2003. The typical antelope for which this region is famous, called the *bongo,*

the color of butterscotch with uneven pinline white stripes running vertically up and down the body. Africa's tiniest antelope, called the *sumi*. Those other antelope, the size of a Chihuahua dog, known as the *dik-dik*. Four extraordinary cheetahs, part of a rehabilitation program for the depleted gene pool we mentioned earlier, in connection with the Serengeti. The shy waterbuck with its musky scent and thick, curly hair. Vervet and Sykes and Colobus monkeys with their lovely collars of frizzy hair, a baby camel, Jackson's *francolin*, Hartlaub's *turaco,* gray parrot. There were porcupine with the long, stiff hair on their heads and stunning black-and-white quills. Contrary to popular belief they do not launch their quills in an attack but rather back into their enemies. The quills come out by themselves and lodge in the victim's flesh; they are difficult and painful to remove. These darts, about thirty centimeters long, are really very handsome: thick, hollow and rather firm to the touch. The Masai and Kikuyu incorporate pieces of them into their jewelry.

We are particularly taken by the caracal cat (African lynx), abandoned as a cub when its mother was killed. It lost the tip of one pointed ear with the tuft of hair on the end and has a bone deficiency as a result of infant malnutrition. This is being treated with a dietary calcium supplement. It paces up and down, just like a domestic cat in a cage, talks to me, rubs its back on the mesh and stares at me with deep longing in the large, hazel eyes. It simplifies Africa to claim that we anthropomorphize the animals, that our responses are really a projection of our sympathies to our own mascots at home, but anyone who knows animals can verify the qualities humans acquired along the evolutionary ladder, perhaps the best of what we presume to claim as our "humanity". Not anthropomorphizing at all.

It starts to rain. The tip of the mountain is veiled in silk and the dragonflies emerge on gossamer wings. The drops let up soon enough and the call of the peacock invites the sun to come out, refreshed and washed clean. My casual stroll back to my cottage, however, is soon interrupted by a clattering of small, hard hooves and the desperate call of the orphanage keeper to head off a baby bongo, escaped and now galloping across the lawn. He has toppled the fence that protects the herb garden, uprooted a bed of roses, veered across the mesh and tools set aside for the construction of a newer and larger aviary and has now found himself near the stables, cornered at the right-angle junction of two hedges. Three bus boys from the hotel kitchen have joined us and now a gardener appears, with a coil of heavy rope. We try to form a barrier to contain the terrified little bongo calf but he breaks through our ranks, tears across the lawn and dodges behind the house used by the "Safari Boutique" under a grove of jacaranda trees dripping with ferns. The mass of lilac blooms, dislodged by the rain, carpets the grass. The bongo slips on the jacaranda petals, skids into the mud and hurtles on.

The two ladies from Detroit we spoke with earlier, on their way to Samburu just north of here, stare in stupefied horror as the ragged platoon gallops past, the lurching little bongo followed by the the rest of us. My camera swings wildly from around my neck but there is never an opportunity to photograph this travesty, a cross between a round-up and the Marx Brothers. The pursuit continues across the grassy slope near the bar, that drops down to the pool, while geese and ibis flee in every direction. The impeccably manicured bowling green becomes just so much trampled turf.

5.

CAROL AND BABY BONGO

The unhappy baby bongo is finally cornered near the employees' quarters. The rope digs into his flesh. He is covered with mud and jacaranda petals. A cut on his muzzle begins to ooze red. A supply truck is brought around and we haul him on board. I accompany him back to the orphanage corral while I stroke the poor little thing, try to feed him from my hand and talk to him softly. In time the trembling and the shivering quiet down and he nuzzles the palms of my hands, with the grain pellets turning soggy from perspiration; he sighs, and dozes off, a frightened young thing in a hostile world that he will never understand.

Having recovered from the Great Bongo Round-up I resume my aborted walk, across the golf course and past the pub-lounge that serves as the Nineteenth Hole, round the lakes and ponds that make up the water hazards and over the thick grass, damp and spongy with rain, into the mist of the woods. At the edge of the hotel grounds another set of rooms in a long empty building turns out to be a film studio, tucked into a forested copse barely visible from one of a network of roads.

I choose from among these unpaved tracks, past a gate that swings freely on its hinges, and wander down by the river. The air is fresh and moist. The river is swollen with mud and debris and the path is packed and dense with clay. The branches of the low-hanging trees are festooned with ferns and the spider webs are bright with silvery drops like beads or sequins or a spray of diamonds, that scatters as I brush too close.

I suddenly realize I am alone and on foot in a game park. Words like "unwise" or "irresponsible" come to mind. I return to the golf course and then discover, at the aviary, that the macaw is a great conversationalist. For openers, "Hello!" but this is only the beginning. After a really meaningful discussion he finally dismisses me, half an hour later, with a hoarse "Bye-bye!", and there it ends.

The horses are lowing in their stalls. The soft muzzles appear over the tops of their doors, for a pat or a bit of sugar. The geese are roosting and the ibis, like large white flowers, fill the trees. Forests, alive with bird and animal sounds, edge up the slope of the mountain and disappear in the snow and mist. Monkeys on the road stand their ground down to the last millimeter, then swing into the tops of trees, or launch a flying leap into the gullies. A plaintive black kitten mews behind a stone house and reassuring puffs of smoke begin to emerge from the chimneys. The constant call of the peacocks reminds me it's time to dress for dinner.

FRIDAY, OCTOBER 27

After breakfast we assemble our belongings and prepare to depart. We run into two Mexican couples in the lobby. They learned in Switzerland that their Genevan tour company had just gone bankrupt, but came on anyway to Africa. Together we examine the bulletin posted near the cashier's window, verifying the game count as of March, 1989, a total of 3,269 animals, brought in for conservation or protection, which form part of an educational program for youngsters, among other activities of the William Holden Foundation.

Elephant: 148; Zebra: 1856; Eland: 383; Giraffe: 388; Kongoni: 298; Ostrich: 9; Waterbuck: 92; Oryx: 50; Warthog: 40; Hippo: 5.

We return across the Equator to the airfield and move the sheep off the runway as the DeHavilland Twin Otter comes down for us, and for Victoria, my Scorpio *si kukuni yako* and her family, who happened to be returning to Nairobi on the same plane. Upon arrival at Wilson Airport, forty minutes later, I also run into the White Hunter from The Ark, with whom we chat for a few minutes, since we have mutual friends in Mexico. Kenya is becoming very small.

Nairobi looks sprawling, freshly washed by the rain. Our driver, who never told us his name, takes us up to the hotel so we can get into storage and add a few parcels to the suitcases, then drives us to the Carnivore Restaurant, a kind of rotating grill—called *carne al pastor* in Mexico and usually known as *skander* (Alexander) in Turkey and Central Asia—not far from Wilson Airport. This is a large and very popular place, rustic and casual, open-air and roofed with timbers, spread out from the central fire pit over which spits are roasting with assorted cuts of chicken, pork, beef, camel, gazelle, ribs, sausage, topi, crocodile, wildebeest, zebra, usually all piled at random on top of each other depending on what is available, with condiments, desserts and plenty of coffee. There are no measured portions. You eat as much or as little as you like.

A private party was in progress in the garden, probably a diplomatic affair judging from the variety of garments, everything from sarong to sari. We might have been in any capital anywhere in the world, but this is Nairobi. A nearby monument attests to a quarter century of "liberation" and the arid countryside around us, just forming, with the rains, a new soft down of pale green, provides the raw material for the richly varied menu.

We return to the airport and a flight of forty-five minutes on one of Air Kenya's two reclaimed and reconstructed Second World War DC-3's, bound for *Kichwa Tembo* or "Elephant Head", the luxury tented camp, named for the jutting promontory behind it which does, certainly, look like an elephant head, abutting on the vast, freckled plain known as the Masai Mara. This is really the northern extension on the Kenyan side, corresponding to the Tanzanian Serengeti to the south, and lies rather near the corner of Lake Victoria that belongs to Kenya, bordering on neighboring Uganda. Not even *close* to Ripon Falls and the emergence of the White Nile from the gigantic lake, no chance of even a *peek* at the birth of the river.

We are met by a pleasant, attractive girl named Asha, hostess for the lodge; and by a full-blooded Masai, raised by Jesuits, named Linus, our guide and driver. He is much more worldly than Eliud, more sophisticated and articulate, and takes full advantage of the Mara's liberal restrictions regarding the trails, zipping his Land Rover in every direction, even to setting us in the middle of a herd of grazing buffalo. They stared and huffed a bit, then returned to their dinner, as world-weary and cosmopolitan as Linus.

The camp faces the woods where the baboon and elephant play, surrounded by an electric fence but in effect, lies within the park. The main building, a stylized extension of a Masai hut, is the reception area, the shop, dining room and lounge, all open to a soft and easy garden, with bougainvillea everywhere, trumpet vines—called "Angels' Trumpet", possibly a response to the narcotic, and potentially lethal, effect when the flowers are soaked and then boiled as an herbal infusion—and a great variety of succulents, to frame the strange juxtaposition of frangi-pani and cactus, or the swimming pool tucked away and hidden in a rocky grotto.

The rows of green coated-canvas tents extend to the left and right of this central area. Each is set on a stone and concrete foundation and is therefore virtually impervious to vipers and vermin.

The tents are about three or four meters apart, for the greater illusion of privacy. They consist in a terrace with a folding table and camp chair on either side of a zippered door-flap, and this vantage point serves very well for early-morning tea, as well as the view across the Mara to the grazing buffalo, giraffe and gazelle, only a short distance away.

Inside is a sleeping area, tastefully furnished with two beds, folding benches at their foot and a headboard which also serves as a night table, with an effective reading light, definitely a novelty. This forms part of a well-designed cabinet with integrated cupboard and closet, and all done in varnished rattan, hand-made in Nairobi. Another zippered flap leads to the bathroom, with its modular plastic stall shower, rattan towel rack and a resourceful dressing-table with mirror into which the sink is set, but which provides generous counter space.

There is also a chemical flush toilet, running water originally heated out back by a wood fire, now replaced by a solar unit, connected to oil drum storage tanks. Electricity in both the overhead fixtures and the reading lamps. The latter, for atmosphere, are converted kerosene lanterns. Sheets are clean and new. Wool blankets keep out the chill of the night and the grunting of the lions at dawn.

We are off on a game drive. The Land Rover is completely open with only a roll bar to hang on to over the ruts and bumps, and we are clinging like khaki-clad sailors bounding across a grassy sea, standing unsteadily and leaning over the edge, not to watch the flying fish go by but the topi with the charcoal smudges on their rumps and under their forelegs, standing by their babies. These unusual antelope are only found on this plain, from the Mara to Serengeti.

Birds soar, close to the ground, taunting a black-maned lion with flies on his muzzle, then into the sky, darting beyond his full belly and his two females, drowsing and dull. If we reach just a little farther we can almost touch them.

We come across a lion pride in a sheltered glade, where a river, nearly dry, takes a sharp bend. Two females, one male and five cubs, are climbing and tumbling, sharpening the claws of their outsized paws on a convenient tree trunk like any housecat at the edge of a sofa, and playing with the dangling grass and roots, like a kitten frolicking with a ball of yarn.

We have rambled along the trails throughout the entire day, stopping only for a granola bar at noon and the dark is setting in, long past our time limit. We check out of the park and return to the hotel, with its perfumed garden: the sensation of a beach with the sea beyond, stretching away under the stars. Again, the analogy of an ocean.

After dinner I look in the shop. An advertising executive I talked with at the Mt. Kenya Safari Club had highly recommended Beryl Markham's little known collection of short stories, **The Secret Admirer,** which he had bought here. I failed to find it among the books on display so resorted to an assault on the language barrier, with the two brothers in attendance. I had trouble explaining what I wanted. We got as far as "book" with no difficulty but then I show them the older and better known **West With the Night,** and point to the author's name. Abruptly one of the brothers dashes out. He returns almost immediately with the book I want and seems visibly triumphant. He surprised me so, and I was so amazed and deeply touched, that I told him how clever he was and he nearly wept with joy. For the rest of our stay, every time I passed the shop, I was treated to an ecstatic *Jambo! ("Hello!"),* and it became my favorite word.

My new friends went to great lengths, after that, to please me. They found me an autographed copy of **The Great Migration,** and unearthed a rare paper on the Masai Mara game reserve, as well as three necklaces of ceramic birds, simple and charming, that they thought I should buy as gifts. Asha, the lodge hostess, provided an explanation. "When a person gives his soul to another through his eyes it is a great treasure and must be acknowledged or somehow it is put to death."

SATURDAY, OCTOBER 28

We rise at five in the morning and enjoy tea on the little stone terrace of our tent before we are collected for a short drive to "Governor's Camp" and a ride in a hot air balloon.

The dawn is vivid and the plain still shadowy under the remaining stars. A grunting lion nearby celebrates his morning kill. Four balloons are inflated along a knoll at the edge of a wooded copse and passengers are assembled, ten to each basket. Tourism by hot air balloon was still in its infancy, though I had been ballooning before, so I felt knowledgeable and actually quite blasé, perhaps to complement, or compensate for, the breathless excitement of all the others, including Tomás, who was terrified, expectant, eager, dubious, until we were in the air and soaring over the herds running from the shadow and the hiss of the gas jet that shoots into the air, into the hollow interior of the festive and brightly colored stripes of an absurd device that slides and eases and sifts, almost silently, across the early morning sky. Now Tomás is mesmerized. The lion and the giraffe, each at its own pace, stride along beneath us, and a large herd of zebra scurries out of the way, pursued by the inexplicable dark thing that is neither a bird nor a cloud nor a gust of wind.

We come down for a bumpy but well guided landing and no one is hurt. We are on our backs, caught inside the basket, our knees pulled up under our chins, waiting for the signal to climb out. Then the ground crew, which has been following us, staying in touch by walkie-talkie, arrives on the scene, like ants bursting from a nest, to fold up the balloon, tuck it away in its canvas bag, haul the basket into the van, dismantle the lines and disconnect the nearly empty gas tanks. The gas permits the balloon to determine its altitude but the direction it takes is the wind's caprice.

6.

HOT AIR BALLOON IN THE MASAI MARA

Another crew has already set up a camp kitchen on the plain. The winds are usually predictable, according to the season, so they know where to go. Folding tables, low and close to the ground, are being assembled, end to end. The gas tanks, laid on their sides, will serve as benches, covered only with green tarpaulin by way of upholstery. Each pilot first brings out a set of metal chalices, then pops the cork on the bottles of Australian champagne. Orange juice, as well, for the Mimosas. They seem the wiser course.

Soon we are lined up, in jovial camaraderie, on either side of our breakfast table, devouring mountains of sliced fresh pineapple, well-done scrambled eggs, roasted Canadian bacon, heaps of thick and succulent sausage, fried bread, sliced tomatoes, butter, mustard, grapefruit marmalade, Kenya cheddar cheese and dark, strong Kenyan coffee with fresh cream. What would Stanley and Livingstone have given for a meal like this!

Peter, our pilot from South London, very solemn and serious, who knows his business, casually and indifferently slips off his overalls to reveal polio-stunted legs in Bermuda shorts. Another pilot, John, a jaunty and seemingly carefree Yorkshireman who feels guilty about "his good life", most of which he spends drinking at "The Parrot Bar" at the Nyali Beach Hotel in Mombasa, teases the "kite" birds with scraps of food, which they wrench from his hands and mouth, but without injury. They know each other. He is showing off. He has singled out the four college girls on holiday who happened to ride in the basket of his balloon.

The other two pilots, both British, were brought out here to fly for the balloon company, owned by one Englishman, one Masai and one Greek. They live a glamorous life, much like the jazz musicians I used to know, who picked up girls from the front line tables in the club; or swimming or tennis instructors, always on the prowl, who single out their targets from among their students. Girls today are more predatory and aggressive. The pilots would be the prey,

The long, bumpy drive back from breakfast on the plain reminds us how far we drifted on the wind and how vast the Mara really is. We stop at a Masai village on the way and arrange with the elders to visit. This is neither a tedious nor a difficult negotiation and is settled with either money, worn-out tennis shoes and t-shirts, or both.

A stockade of brush and thorns, at least three meters high, protects the circle of huts and the round dirt enclosure within. This is trampled and dried, then dampened from the rain or the urine of dozens of head of cattle, and trampled again, carpeted with dung— which is used, as in India, rural Iran or Syria, Afghanistan, Central Asia—both for stucco and for fuel, and is alive with millions of flies.

A few young boys of about five or six play in the dirt with the youngest calves, that have been left behind from the day's grazing. An assortment of dogs, mangy curs all of them, huddle in on themselves as if they were cold, though the sun is high and strong. Each hut is

occupied by a woman and her children and often her older relatives—
a mother or an aunt—who occupies one of the compartmented areas
inside the windowless and round wattle-and-daub dwelling.

Architecture varies from region to region and so does the shape
of the huts, which may be oval, round or almost rectangular and are
less diminutive than they initially appear from a distance. Grimy
and stained plastic containers for water, which may also be used
for cow's milk, lie about, along with broken wooden stools or a tattered garment. Many of the small boys are wearing t-shirts with
"Superman" on them or some equally unequivocal reminder of the
invasion of a society that has no cultural application, really, to these
people's own heritage.

Adult women, wrapped in their layers of crimson plaid, checked
or solid red cloth, their heads shaved and their jewelry of glass or
wooden beads in luxuriant masses around their necks, stand in
attendance next to a display of their crafts, in case there might be
an odd sale or two. Most of them are pregnant or have little girls,
dressed much like themselves, in hand at their sides.

Both men and women have elongated earlobes, that have been
flayed and stretched until the lobe itself is a kind of dangling ear
ring which swings freely, independently of the head. The features,
however, are invariably fine and elegant, and have never been
altered. There is no tattooing or scarring, neither to face nor body.
The aristocratic noses, the beautifully chiseled lips, the well-shaped
eyes set into the smallish head in the stylish, lean proportion of the
fashion model, all conform to a refined aesthetic and have been left
as nature designed them, though they have surely been subjected
to female genital mutilation, known as "female circumcision", companion to the early commitments to arranged marriages, often
among blood relatives, along with the health hazards and physical
strain of premature motherhood.

A reference to the practice of "ablation"—whose technique and
severity vary according to the tribe and its customs—ostensibly

appears on the sarcophagus of Sit-hedjhotep dating from ancient Egypt's Middle Kingdom, c. 1991-1786 B.C., and was described by Strabo (c. 64 B.C.-c. 23 B.C.), who visited Egypt early in the first century B.C. *"This is one of the customs most zealously pursued by these Egyptians, applied to every child that is born, thus circumcising the males and excising the females."*

Greek philosopher Philo of Alexandria (c. 20 B.C.-50 B.C.) added that *"the Egyptian practice conforms to God's commandment as put forth in the Book of Genesis, dating from roughly nine centuries ago, that boys be circumcised as they begin to get seed, and females a menstrual flow, in their approximately fourteenth year, in order to curb venality and restrain population excess."*

Two men stand about, coated in red blankets, leaning on their spears and dressed as any other Masai herdsmen, except for the tattered tennis shoes on the leathery feet. They are doing guard duty today. Women are generally regarded as fragile, useless except for domestic duties and helpless in a crisis. The men therefore rotate and are on hand if a child is hurt, if a predator or a stranger appears inside the stockade or if someone is cut with a rusty knife. They pass the morning keeping an eye on things while the women and children look out for the aged, or for the chickens, calves and puppies, the very young or the very old. What would happen in a real emergency? Are there disinfectants or bandages? Or is there even clean water to wash a wound? Not at first glance.

The villagers live on the products of their cattle. They pierce a vein under the ear of a cow and extract enough blood to mix with the milk; this serves as nourishing sustenance. As for meat, they cut a slab off the rump, pack the wound with mud and let it heal, just as James Bruce had seen in Ethiopia in the eighteenth century despite the disbelief of the European readers of his reports, thus preserving the animal for another day.

The encroachment of other tribes in this area, explains Linus, our driver, has encouraged agriculture and a diversification of the diet, "but for many centuries," he says, "the Masai lived in isolation and kept not only their customs but their values intact, as well as their high estimation of a peaceful life, their capacity for love and for tribal integrity, along with their much-admired independence." Linus, whose Masai name is *Tompoy*, says he has no conflict where national loyalty is concerned. He considers that his citizen responsibility is totally separate from his tribal identification, and this again has no bearing, he says, on the Catholicism acquired through his Jesuit education.

"The Europeans who arrived here and decided to stay," Linus goes on, "preserved a part of their puritanical heritage, their class structure and racism, but they were also seduced by the enormous equatorial sun in a magnificent, limitless sky, by the stars and the freedom, the insinuation of danger, whether real or imagined. They applied their pioneering spirit to the ethereal in Africa, the unstructured, the intangible, the morally exotic. Just like 'Johnny the baboon pilot', as the Yorkshireman calls himself, they could never get over the guilt of the good life and the underlying sensation of Hell to pay, but who cares?"

These settlers, Linus continues, found a compensation in hard bargains and hard work, calloused hands, shrewd deals, in order to convince themselves that they were entitled to remain, that it belonged to them because they loved it so, and had worked so hard, and they sold themselves on the idea of the unworthiness of the natives, who "if left to their own devices would run it to wrack and ruin." So for the Europeans, Africa prospered on a European scale, by European standards. "This becomes increasingly hard to accept, as I watch the Masai villagers, caught in a 'progress' they neither believe in nor will they benefit from, while they drive their herds of cattle and goats in serene unconcern."

The wildebeest turn as we pass. They have stayed on with their zebra friends well into the rainy season. Now we are tearing across open country. Two cheetahs lie by the road. They have eaten so much they are incapable of action. They just pant, their bellies vibrating in rhythm, and watch us, the tear marks neatly drawn on their tiny heads, the eyes large and golden in a piercing stare. These are the only ones among the great cats that hunt by sight rather than scent. Their phenomenal speed compensates for their smaller size and lesser weight and the fact that their claws are not retractable.

A black speck appears in the distance, growing larger as it approaches. Its gait is steady and implacable, varying neither in course nor in speed. It turns out to be a solitary wild dog, or hunting dog, a rare sight since they usually run in a pack and are increasingly threatened with extinction.

Sure enough, two more follow about five hundred meters behind the leader. He seems to know exactly where he wants to go and we turn the Land Rover about to follow him onto the dusky horizon. He is relentless and never seems to tire. His strategy is clear as we come upon the single Thomson's gazelle, applying a futile spurt of desperate speed. The wild dog brings it down in mid-flight and before it hits the ground has already torn open the chest. He has begun to devour the tender organs while the gazelle, still alive, thrashes on the ground. The spleen, the lungs, the heart. The wild dog is gorging himself before the other two arrive and he will regurgitate his kill to feed his young. When food is scarce the wild dog will give preference to his pups, since he normally uses them to run down a prey; they play an active role in the hunt. On the other hand the lion, in lean times, will deprive his cubs until they die off, leaving the food supply for the adults, who keep the larder full. They can always breed new cubs later, when the pantry again overflows.

The wild dog is actually inside the chest cavity of the still-warm gazelle, whose carcass moves in jerky spasms from the tearing at its innards. The other two arrive. They are wearing radio collars, and are obviously being tracked by scientists in the area. The dogs' dinner is confined to the flesh under the skin as their friend already beat them to the choice morsels. When they are satisfied they trot away, to make room for the tawny eagles and the vultures.

Linus is intoxicated with speed and the night. We bounce over large boulders and thorn bushes, across gullies, around the knolls and into the washes of dry rivers, that will soon, with the rains, rush in flash flood. The damp scent of rain comes up behind us, as we scatter a shy herd of waterbucks and a baby giraffe. The African night is dense, panting and vast. It seems never to end. The sky is wider here, the stars brighter. The shades of blue turn nearly green and black.

SUNDAY, OCTOBER 29

The African dawn is darker, even, than the night, black velvet turned then to transparent pink silk, laid over a soft French blue. The muffled croaking of the frogs and the scrambling of the aardvark become the happy chatter of monkeys and the manic birds. Tea and biscuits are served on the terrace of the tent. A large cat in the lobby of the hotel, pregnant and friendly, purrs as we pass. Every hotel has one.

As we depart for our morning game drive I can see the balloons taking off in the distance. Elephant are feeding in the woods and a topi has caught the eye of a hungry lioness on her dawn prowl. She is joined by a sister and they set up a stake-out, fifty meters apart, almost hidden by the tall grass. The topi trots away to a safe distance. A huge troop of baboons stalks out to greet the morning.

We cross a deserted plain, enter a dry wash and come out on the grassland beyond. In all we have driven over three hundred kilometers, up and down on the Mara, while the wart hog, topi, waterbuck and buffalo go about their business, and will continue to do so long after we have gone.

The gazelle are everywhere this morning. About two hundred of them are born each day, to satisfy the appetite of the carnivores and to maintain the population balance in the park. We stumble by an abandoned termite mound, grown over and toppling. There is a soft chill in the air. A film of clouds is strung across the sun. We are of good appetite when we return to the lodge, for one of those hearty breakfasts of local fruits and fresh juice, crepes, eggs, fried round rings of bread like miniature doughnuts, doughy croissants, juicy thick sausage and bacon, canned baked beans, cold and hot cereals, fresh milk, coffee and tea.

Our flight back to Nairobi departs at mid-morning. When the plane is near it radios the hotel, in time to collect the passengers and their gear and herd them out to the runway, only five minutes away, which must then be cleared of topi, gazelle and wart hog; they flee in all directions.

After landing, and the disgorging of the incoming passengers, the departing few resort to a certain amount of pushing and shoving as they crowd around a stewardess—a service we had only encountered on the Mara flight—looking for their names on a list. This process amounts to a check-in counter. The pilot and co-pilot, both black Kenyans, toss our bags into the hold and the DC-3 takes off, while we wave goodbye to Asha and Linus.

We make a stop at Keekorok Camp for more passengers while an ostrich, the burnished plains behind him, watches us frozen in disbelief. His eyes never blink. His enormous claws are clutched and sunk into the ground. Only the soft feathers of his breast and tail ruffle in the faint breeze, then flap madly as the wind stirred up by the departing plane blows across him.

As we approach Wilson Airport, over the shantytown sprawl, the city in the distance, we somehow perceive the Masai Mara differently. It must be relegated to the yearning of my most secret heart or I might go mad in the longing for it. If I hunger too much for the scent of the grass, the pungent dampness before dawn, the red fringe around the blue velvet sky, the animals strewn across the plains, I might find the half-forgotten child I used to be, the hiding places of my infancy, the phrase in a poem, a melancholy song.

Then it evaporates, or does it? This undefined rapture. It will reappear in an unsuspected and perhaps dangerous disguise, but that is later. Now it is Sunday in the city. We are home.

$$\int\int\int$$

Nairobi on a Sunday afternoon, with puddles still standing in the streets, is nearly deserted. Only by the market where the disheartened beggars gather, or in the milling about of people near the mosque, or among the ladies in flowered hats coming out of church, is there any sign of vitality under the lowering clouds.

"African Heritage" and the downtown hotels, on the other hand, are lively, and we plan to look in after a stop at the Nairobi Safari Club, to reassemble the heavy luggage in the storage room. I find a bellboy not too busy to unlock the door but he has a call so turns away and I become too preoccupied to notice. When I have repacked, however, and carefully stacked the suitcases on the rack, I try the door and it is locked. The first sensation is one of panic but quiet reasoning determines that there must be a telephone. By following the cord from the connection near the door I find it half-hidden under soft parcels left by a careless tourist, or tossed there by a thoughtless bellboy. I phone for the operator but have a certain amount of difficulty making my situation clear. I am put through to the concierge's desk, but the person who picks up the phone has trouble understanding me. He catches the word suitcase and puts me through to the travel desk, where an employee thinks he has received a mistaken call and hangs up. I start all over again. It must have been clearer the second time because in a few moments I hear the key in the lock and see a worried smile, like a bright light, across the dark face.

After iced tea in the lounge we go out for a walk. The idlers and the shoe-shine boys near one of the mosques begin to rave about my shoes which are, in effect, something very special. They fit perfectly and my feet never tire. I am not clear, however, whether they hope to buy them, for me to make a gift of them or simply want me to submit to a polish job, which I decline.

We are looking for a shop, Aquarius, recommended by a lady at Kichwa Tembo, for amber, for mineral stone beads and for coin-silver Ethiopian crosses, but it is closed on Sunday. We ended in the coffee shop at the Intercontinental Hotel and ran into a honeymoon couple from Canada who had been in our basket on the balloon ride. They raved about those triangular turnovers called *samosas,* originally from India, that we were only too happy to try.

We were to be in the train station at five for departure on the overnight "iron snake" bound for Mombasa. The station at that time was located not far from the Railroad Museum and the relic locomotives from the Uganda Railroad, later reconditioned and refurbished for filming in *Out of Africa.*

7.

MOMBASA BOUND ON THE UGANDA RAILWAY

Our own train was reasonably modern, though it had surely seen better and fresher days. Tomás may never forgive me for that train ride. We had a drawing room. A sink, covered with a hinged top, occupied one corner and I think there was a ladder to reach the top bunk but we never used it. Tomás, who is claustrophobic, took the bottom bunk, and I simply used the corner sink as a step to reach the upper.

I remember feeling very close and short of air up there during the night and trying to get out without disturbing Tomás. I put my foot over the side, ignoring the ladder and aiming for the more accessible covered sink—which was so dirty no one was ever going to use it—and in so doing knocked over two bottles of soda water, while I fell against the division to the adjacent drawing room, bashing it open, swearing all the time. Then I was tossed into the door of the passageway by the lurching of the train.

It was not one of our more successful choices of transport. Our bedding, which we rented for an additional forty shillings above the price of passage, was clean enough but persistently slipped on the cracked and worn leather of the bunks. The dining car, a haggard relic of a long-departed era, was a marvel: waiters still wearing the now tattered and threadbare remains of the original East Africa Railroad Company livery. A photograph dated 1898 of a bygone Board of Directors, which included the mean and ruthless Sir Robert Beaumont played by Tom Wilkinson in *The Ghost and the Darkness,* still hung on the oak-paneled wall. Flatware consisted in an assortment of the original silver pieces, still bearing the worn initials of the rail company. Waiters, however, were careless, or not observant enough, to lay a table with a complete setting, so antiques had been combined with more modern stainless steel or silver plate, to fill the gaps. The food was terrible. A clear soup was served in a broad, open soup bowl, in total disregard for the lurching, which was probably a blessing, because it spilled and we didn't have to eat it. But the dishes were also the original bone china, or what remained of it, mostly chipped. The waiter's grinning face beamed even more brightly when he heard we were from Mexico. "I read in the paper about your problems there. I am so sorry." We explained that the problems he referred to had to do with Panama, not Mexico, but he was unconvinced.

The kitchen was also the original, as were the paneling and the light fixtures, with their fringed shades. The flooring was coming up and we could see the tracks flying along under our feet, as we sidestepped the holes. It had been a triumph of tenacity to build this railroad. Workers were attacked as they tried to string the telegraph cables, monkeys and baboons climbed the poles and giraffes would either strangle on the lines or simply snap them off, then wander the plain with the dangling wires around their necks.

The route, after leaving behind the fetid Kibera shantytown, runs along the boundary of Nairobi National Park. There are hundreds of stops, at every village, settlement and community along the way, from Embakasa on. In the late afternoon light we can see the giraffe in the distance, the zebra and buffalo. In the shadows and smudges of the darkening night the Grant's gazelle come into view, vultures and eagles, squalid train stations and the vast landscape. Eager children clamor at the sides of the train under our open window, hoping for money or sweets, and wildebeest appear on the horizon. Dark falls just after stony Athi, on the river of the same name. We catch the scent of wood smoke.

During the frequent stops the breeze freshens from the window, carrying the disquieting aroma of the African night. Foreigners somehow tend to become enamored, even intoxicated, by the immensity of Kenya and abandon all prudence and moderation. I was to remember this later and to carry it with me for a long time.

The sky is flung open like a banner or a pair of jubilant arms unfurled. There are still cerulean patches between the clouds, which are turning dove gray and steel, until they finally become soft charcoal, enveloped in the scent of the endless grass.

We eventually get to bed, with the intention of sleep, and do, in fact, doze off in stages. The night is long, with many stops and at one point, a torrential rain.

MONDAY, OCTOBER 30

It is just after dawn. The toilet is a disaster. Prohibited its use while standing in a station, it is equally useless while the train is in motion. The wind whistles through the open hole and the tracks are clearly visible through the aperture. How do the other passengers solve this? The filthy, covered sink comes to mind.

During the night we traveled right down the middle of Tsavo Game Park, over the Tsavo River. Stephen Hopkins directed the 1996 film, from a script by William Goldman, that tells the story of Irish engineer John Henry Patterson's beautiful bridge, contracted by Beaumont of the firm assigned the task of building the equatorial rail line. The project is mysteriously haunted by the two rogue lions that torment the crew, until Patterson (Val Kilmer) manages to shoot them. Their badly preserved remains are on display in the Field Museum of Natural History in Chicago where I went to see them for myself. During the train ride we saw nothing.

Now we are approaching the lush Indian Ocean coast. Outside the window are orange groves, bananas, tattered and shaggy coconut palms, gigantic mango trees, papaya—here called "paw-paw"—and flame trees, tamarind and the stiff palms of the *coyol* or "oil nut".

"This is Papaloapan," insists Tomás. Brightly-colored birds whistle through the trees, there is water everywhere.

We pass the Caltex oil refinery and fields of cane and corn. Bougainvillea, in every imaginable color, frames the route. The train is chugging along very slowly. In Changamwe we pass an evangelists' mission school, and then cross over a web of waterways, of inlets and islands, that turns out to be Akamba, of the craft cooperative, to which we will return later in the day. For the moment we are pulling into Mombasa Station. It is seven in the morning. The express train, which left Nairobi before ours, is due to arrive at ten.

The waiting room is divided into first and second classes but outside, on the plaza facing the station, there are mobs of people, of no particular distinction. Not only people: trucks, buses, horns honking and turmoil. Indian women in sari, Muslim women draped in black *chador*, local women of languorous gait in brightly colored cotton, bundles of fibers and brooms, parcels and buckets quivering on their heads. Men in white shirts with sweat stains underarm, puddles, smelly engines of overworked cars, the cloying rot of the copra and the fish drying in the sun.

Our driver identifies himself and scurries us into a waiting vehicle, then takes us back up to Akamba to watch the artisans fashion animals from the precious hardwoods—ebony, mahogany, cedar, musheragi, muiri, mukeo, camphor, and musaise, using the grain as part of the design. Craft, yes, but aspiring to art. Three hundred men in an assembly line procedure of literally hundreds of thousands of wood carvings. The thatched shelters are laid out in rows along paths that act as streets and inside, the men are aligned like galley slaves, intent on one or another of the processes: removing the excess outer wood, outlining the figure in relief, modeling, polishing or applying a stain, especially to the giraffe's blotches or the leopard's spots, by flaming.

8.

AKAMBA WOODCARVER, TOMÁS IN THE BACKGROUND

The figures are not sculptures, the skill is dubious, the spontaneity absent, as would be expected of a process only really effective for producing automobiles in Detroit, yet something of tradition seeps through, something of inherent inspiration, every animal and every tribe appears in every possible shape and position. The men work with hands as well as feet, even to putting backs and entire bodies into their effort. Head down, neck turned, shoulders bent, legs crossed, feet locked, grand, withdrawn, like their wooden figures: they are solid, ethereal, stoic, disdainful, flirtatious, involved, absent; they are alone or in groups of two or three. It seems a great waste of so many trees to invest the lives of so many men in so mediocre an enterprise.

Mombasa was then an island, in fact, a network of islands, interlaced by canals, joined by bridges. In the low-tide debris Mombasa is a symphony of odors, embraced by the surrounding mangroves, swamps and channels, of burning garbage, drying nets, whirring pelicans and outraged gulls. An offshore reef protects the entrance to both the old and the new harbors. The city was then a tapestry, of British Colonial and resort modern, of Hindu temples and green-and-white mosques, of public markets and dark green parks, *baobab* trees and a dreadful monument downtown, of two gigantic stylized tusks forming a grimy white concrete arch over the main street.

We drive up to a bluff overlooking the South Port where the ferries dock and I thought I saw a baby crocodile dart into the underbrush but it was only a monitor lizard, nomadic and vagrant, scooting away under my feet. The park is alive with cashew vendors, frangi-pani blooms, the coastline melting into the mangroves and a brightly decorated Casino.

The really interesting part of the city is the Old Port, near Fort Jesus, right out of Joseph Conrad, Melville or Hall, of lost souls and safe harbors, storms and tillers and rotting timbers, turbaned stevedores, coiled ropes, bundles wrapped in hemp whose seams are sewn with cord, dhows at anchor and chains and tarnish and rust. Worry beads and warehouses, traders, brokers shrouded in tobacco smoke calculating their commission, stray cats, stray sailors hoping for a berth, stray cargo, the wealth of the world, spices and gold.

The port is closed to casual visitors. This is a Muslim community and we are infidels, though we believe in God. To them it is another God and we are not welcome. And yet they tolerate us. We stroll along the twisting streets, under Portuguese balconies and steep stairways, shops that smell of incense, silver jewelry, silk, salty heat, sifting sand and the scent of the pale green sea.

Fort Jesus, *Forte Jesus de Mombaça,* that corroded web of coral and stucco, when seen from the air was built in the shape of a man. It stands on a spur of pure coral overlooking the harbor. Vasco da Gama first sailed into Mombasa in 1498, just after Columbus had claimed America for the Spanish. After only one week, however, what with Muslim animosity, he thought it more prudent to move on to friendlier Malindi, just up the coast. There the Portuguese established their first East African stronghold.

Mombasa's natural harbor nonetheless attracted an Ottoman expedition, that in 1589 built a fort for its protection. The Portuguese were understandably upset. They feared for the security of their route back to the Atlantic, as well as their trade lanes into the Arabian Sea, so under orders from King Philip I of Portugal (King Philip II of Spain) attacked Mombasa after all, and despite the Ottoman cannons, with naval power superior to the Turks', secured it in 1593. They incidentally also considered themselves the bastion of Christianity and sailed under the flag of the Order of Christ. Jesus was therefore an obvious choice as a name for their new fort, whose angular form, constructed from 1593-1596, was not only dictated by the essentials of military defense but also by the creative criterion of Milanese architect Giovanni Battista Cairati, master designer of the constructions in Portugal's Eastern holdings, imported for this purpose from their colony in Goa.

Between 1631 and 1875 the fort was put to siege, defended, lost and won again, in all nine times, by the powers contesting control of the splendid harbor, the most important on Africa's Indian Ocean coast. Britain, which used the fort as a prison, ordered the construction of the railroad in 1898 to connect Mombasa with the interior. In 1958 the Fort was declared a national monument and in 2011 a UNESCO World Heritage Site.

Fort Jesus is now a museum and monument, displaying the relics of a long history of murder, siege, starvation, bombardment, commerce and treachery, a defender of a tiny colony in a hostile world, with rusted cannons, salvage from shipwrecks, elaborately carved wooden doors from Oman, trading beads from Venice, chests from Persia, jewelry from Zanzibar, and bits of Chinese export pottery, once the ballast of every ocean-going vessel until replaced by English porcelain.

We drive out of town and up the coast, to the Nyali Beach Hotel, a sprawling resort, obviously the holiday choice for the Europeans in Nairobi, with several bars and restaurants, shops, two swimming pools, tennis and water sports and "Parrot's", a beach bar facing the reef.

After a long walk on the windy beach, nearly as far as the channel into Mombasa Island, we return to shower, rinse out clothes and dress for dinner. Veronica, my Scorpio friend from the Mt. Kenya Safari Club, had insisted we make reservations to dine at the Tamarind, the Mombasa branch of the Nairobi restaurant and, faithful to our promise, since we had been warned not to wander around at night, we hired a taxi for the occasion.

The restaurant lies on a bluff overlooking a quiet cove, with a view of the city's lights, spilling their reflections down into the lapping water. A large excursion dhow is tied up at a wooden dock below. The Tamarind, back then, was only a roof and open sides, a dance floor and drinks on the terrace, under a pergola of night-blooming jasmine, with a fireworks display opposite, across the channel.

We had already been precisely instructed: the mangrove crab and rich Kenyan coastal lobster are the finest in the world and there can be no doubt as to the wisdom of the advice. The diner is provided with a wooden club to batter the shells. The finger bowls are clay buckets hanging from metal tripods, brought to the table with bath towels. I would be more than willing to return to Mombasa, just to order the same dinner, but as we said before, in another syntax and context, "some things are better remembered than imagined". The moon was rising, drums were beating, fireworks and starlight reflecting in the harbor: no use arguing with pure magic.

TUESDAY, OCTOBER 31

We are awake and about, it's four in the morning, our flight time was moved up a full hour. Just as well, as we were reminded later.

This way we would have another full day in Lamu. Dawn reflects the colors of the coral on the offshore reef, barely visible through the haggard fronds of the flapping coconuts.

We check in at the counter of a small, excursion airline called "Prestige", at the entrance to Mombasa's very modern Moi International Airport, and are led inside and ceremoniously deposited in a large waiting room by a girl in black skirt and white blouse, a clipboard clutched to her chest. The Piper will not board, she reminds us, until all the passengers have arrived and are available, and this troubles Tomás, who wants his breakfast. Those banquet breakfasts in the game parks are habit forming.

A German businessman appears, ten minutes late and with a rumpled collar, tie askew, and the three of us are guided out onto the tarmac, where we board the tiny plane. Our young pilot was born in New Jersey but there is no opportunity to ask him how he got to the Kenya coast.

It had been drizzling but now clears and a rainbow appears: a good omen. We take off over Mombasa Island with its waterways and lagoon, waves breaking over the reef and, beyond, the Indian Ocean, green and flat. We are flying now over Malindi, with its resorts and oceanographic institute. Nyali Beach disappears in the distance. The reef breaks off and long waves roll toward a jagged shore. A network of bays and lagoons turns the coastline to lace; and a dhow, driven southwest by the *Kaskazy,* that legendary coastal wind, runs past two observation platforms used for marine research.

The mangrove swamps shelter a number of dune-lined islands with fluted sand beaches, like chunks broken off the shore. Lamu is one of these, a rhomboid that fits, a perfect piece from a complex jigsaw puzzle, inside the frill of the reappeared reef. Next to it is Manda, another island, with the landing strip of coral pebbles, over which the Piper bumps to a halt. Our bags are taken off and we look around for the person who was supposed to meet us. A swarm of swarthy Swahil and Bantu boys promises that no one will come. It is not the custom. We are to take a boat across the channel to Lamu town, where the Lamu Express will ferry us the three kilometers down the channel to Peponi's Hotel behind the dunes near the beach.

Off we went, followed by the boys, in a jaunty parade, the half kilometer to the jetty, which is broken. We had to scramble under the pilings along a walkway encrusted with barnacles, bumping our heads and fuming, to reach the small dhow, and then sail across the channel: blue water, blue sky, Muslim boys with bare feet and white knitted caps, batik-dyed cloth wrapped around their bodies from the waist down, beneath the tattered t-shirts they had inherited from departing tourists.

The dhow is small, no more than a dinghy with a triangular sail and a wide beam. There is no place to stand and only a bench along the bulwark for sitting, keeping the head down to avoid a smack from the mangrove-rod boom when the able little boatman tacks and brings it around. There are few women, but all of them are Muslim, encased in black *chador* that flutter in the sea breeze. They were terrified of having their picture taken. They watched us with dark eyes wide, but with one hand on the side of the boat, to steady themselves, and the other clutching their *chador* across their faces.

The town took shape across the channel. It seemed low and modest, until we reached a hopelessly inadequate and obsolete dock, where dhows were tied up in parallel lines, so that people in the outer boats could cross over the nearer ones to reach the ladders and stairs. Bundles and parcels were stacked on the dock, cases of beer and soft drinks, and sacks of flour and sugar being brought out of the hold of an ocean-going dhow by stevedores in headbands and dripping with sweat, their arms sleek and brown, their bodies lean, the muscles taut.

Ferries filled with women in black, who peek at us from under their *chador*, chattered and buzzed, bound for the towns around this or other nearby islands that devote themselves to building dhows, to fishing, or to the cutting of mangrove poles, once Lamu's greatest export product and source of wealth. Dhows at anchor, tipsy and lopsided, or abandoned for repairs, line the shore of the channel.

9.

LAMU WATERFRONT, 1989

Lamu runs along a waterway, at high tide broad and deep, under a grove of beach pines and coconuts, on an otherwise arid and sandy island, with Portuguese balconies on the Iberian wooden houses in the front rank facing the water. Behind them meanders a labyrinth of tiny lanes, with construction fashioned of mud bricks coated with adobe stucco, or the better buildings, of coral block, so close they almost join, with narrow and precarious adobe stairways *outside* the house, that rise to the tiny window or perhaps the wooden balcony on the upper level. This allows the women to gossip and chatter from house to house. From the many mosques the *muezzim,* in a melancholy wail, call the faithful to prayer. *Allah Akbar...*God is indeed great, for bringing us here.

10.

COASTAL VILLAGER ON THE LAMU EXPRESS

The Lamu Express, a dilapidated boat with a chugging engine, runs up and down the channel, ferrying guests to Peponi's or to the small town of Shella just behind the hotel. Around two hundred years ago the population numbered some two thousand in all but now only amounts to approximately seven hundred. The people, we are told, moved away, in the fourteenth century, over to Takwa on the island of Manda, just across the channel, but eventually the water there also went brackish so they moved again, and have been moving ever since.

Shella is being rebuilt. A new mosque is in progress, as the old one is in ruin; and the islanders who devote themselves to the cutting of coral block are doing a brisk business. Unfortunately, the blocks are cut from the very foundation of the islands, so in the strictest sense they are undercutting their own supports, painting themselves into a corner, so to speak. The blocks are treated with lime and then are "roasted" over a mangrove fire, the very technique the Mayas used on the crumbly native stone in Mexico's southern state of Campeche, to treat the building blocks for their temples and palaces. Wells, each time deeper, supply the town's fresh water, as long as it lasts. An ancient brick well, completely abandoned, is still visible on the shore as we chug along the channel.

The shoreline is a living cross-section of the entire region, with an assortment of houses in different styles, depending on who built them or to whom they will be rented: Arab houses with fabulous carved doors

11.

CARVED WOODEN LAMU DOOR

whose owners live part of the year in Oman; German or French houses to be let out to seasonal vacationers; English houses for Europeans who work in the area; African huts for the Swahil families who act as caretakers.

It is 1989, the town has been chosen as the location for the filming of Bob Rafelson's depiction of the William Harrison novel, describing the 1857-58 journey of Richard Francis Burton and John Hanning Speke in their expedition to Central Africa. Lamu is the ideal setting for reproducing the Zanzibar of more than a century earlier, boats being stocked and loaded, bearers, cargo, with a scene portraying Omar Shariff as the Sultan, as well as the starlight attack on the explorers' camp, shot on the dunes.

But when the film company departs the local government orders a new dock, and the wharf along the waterfront is being modernized; Lamu is being rebuilt and remodeled.

12.

BANTU WORKMAN ON THE LAMU CANAL

This may be good and it may be bad. The museum, one of the lovely Portuguese houses on the waterfront, embellished with magnificent carved doors—the famous "Lamu doors"—is being expanded. Open sewage is scheduled to be remedied with new drainage. The obsolete, but utterly enchanting market, or bazaar, will be rebuilt, there will be new schools, a clinic, warehouses, but a part of the old life will be gone. Cruise ships were beginning, even then, to come into the channel and will decidedly alter the traditional way of life, as well as the configuration of the coastline.

There seem to be many young things about: children with runny noses, baby donkeys, hundreds of kittens. The town is literally carpeted with slim cats that look like the Bastet of Egyptian murals, taking the morning sun on every bench and in every doorway. Rotund Indian merchants, burgeoning bellies, legs wide apart, sit behind a wooden table in their shops, working on their accounts. They emigrated generations ago, mostly from Gujurat. The Arabs came from South Arabia, from today's Oman and Yemen, and two hundred years ago there were still a number of Portuguese. Their local version of a Fort, also called Jesus, is being refurbished as a community and cultural center, with an eye toward future tourism. The new pier will have separate areas for passengers and cargo. "This is very necessary," we are told, "as now the women and old men fall into the water."

Many of the ruins of the Swahil (meaning "coastal") towns go back to the ninth century. Even Lamu was larger than it is now, during the climax of its trading period, carefully illustrated in the museum. The dhow was the key to commerce. These hardwood boats with the mangrove mast, carved and polished to bring them to life, are the mainstay of the Indian Ocean. The larger dhows that go to sea or that follow the *Kaskazy* winds down to Malindi and Mombasa, and the fishing dhows near the shore, are equally nimble, and the men who sail them are nothing short of miraculous. The square or triangular sail is completely flexible. Its span depends on the size of the boat. If turned on its side it becomes a spinnaker. The slightest breath of wind is sufficient to slice through the waters; but these shrewd sailors make the best use both of too little or too much wind. They seem unfazed by circumstances of the weather. Seafaring people blended here, in the history of human migration and the discovery of new lands by navigating the oceans of the world, using compass, sextant, astrolabe, long since invented, but mostly by reading the stars and the wind, the currents of the sea, clouds and their colors, the migratory patterns of the birds. Phoenicians, Greeks, Persians, Arabs encountered the Norsemen, the Chinese and the South Pacific Austronesians. They have been a seafaring people all their lives; many of them left logs for those who followed, instructions, specifications. Columbus and Magellan already knew where they were headed.

Behind the town of Lamu, in fact part of it, lies the "African" village, a colony of wattle-and-daub dwellings, the reed supports filled in with clay with coral chinking, and this is where the blacks live. There are no descendants of Indian or Arab traders here, no families of Europeans or children of white settlers. The foreign element prefers being closer to the water yet everyone up and down the coast, black, brown or white, gathers at Peponi's. Even with restaurant, bars and small hotels in the town Peponi's—the white stucco house perched on the rocks above the dunes near the entrance to the channel—is everyone's headquarters.

The rooms, small and functional but unprepossessing, are lined up in a row along the garden, under oleander, coconuts and bougainvillea, with verandas and *chaises longues* facing the channel. This area is entered through a gate from the sandy lane that leads to Shella, behind the hotel. On the other side of the lane is a terrace, with bar and café available to the public. Beyond that is the door to the inner hotel lounge and behind that, the private dining room for hotel guests only. Also for guests is the veranda, mostly for tea, that encloses the tiny inner courtyard with four tables and a flower-draped pergola and, just behind it, a reading room. The office is somewhere beyond, deep in the interior of the rambling structure, that seems to have spread like a weed, without a real pattern or design, but which enjoyed the services, even back then, of a computer, as well as a ship-to-shore radio.

The original owner was Italian, hence the name, but for a long time Peponi's had belonged to a Danish family, whose son, born in Kenya, ran the hotel, along with a Kenya-born English girl, Agatha, who artfully ran the restaurant, and this early in the era of cosmopolitanism in the gastronomic revolution that began in the eighties. The food, usually fish, purchased from the dhows that came up to offer their daily wares, was superb, with great inventiveness in the use of herbs and spices and a genuine flair in the choice of menus.

The manager was surprised to see us. "We expected you much later. How did you get here? Someone was just on his way to pick you up."

We explained that our plane had landed ahead of schedule and that the boys on the landing strip had told us no one would come, so we had enjoyed a fine morning looking around. "Have some breakfast, anyway," he insisted, to Tomás' enormous relief, ordering a table laid. Either we were starving or the food was exquisite, maybe both.

As soon as we had eaten and gotten settled we started off again. I was grateful we had poked around earlier in the day as now the heat was up and it was fierce. We walked back to town, through Shella and along the edge of the channel, by the fish traps, in front of the new hospital—a gift from Saudi Arabia—and the ginner's, where cotton was being unloaded from the dhows pulled up on the shore. The stevedores refused to be photographed and the men repairing the sails of the dhows in dry-dock were equally adamant about being left alone. Their reticence extended to my notebook—"What are you writing? Who are you reporting to?"—so I made mental notes, of the tailor shop, the butcher's, watch repair, the shirt-maker, the grocer, the shop with the silk and cotton cloth from India, and the silver jewelry and the antiques—or maybe not antique but definitely old: the daggers with jeweled handles, the tusks adorned with silk tassels and silver, the famous Lamu trumpets; and then there was the sandal-maker, the shoe repair, the barber, the carpenter and the baker. They all live upstairs, over their shops. The women, in the street, are alien and silent but inside their houses they chatter and giggle and point at us.

We had been told to find "The General", to arrange a boat back to Peponi's. I had planned to walk but Tomás immediately protested that it was too hot. We peered around the dock. Despite the heat there was the same feverish traffic as we had seen in the morning, of unloading bales, bundles, sacks and boxes, the bearers naked down to a tattered loincloth, streaming with sweat, no more covering than a carelessly rolled turban on their heads as a cushion for their load and a cloth hanging down their back, to keep the sun off their necks.

We turned to ask at random for "The General". There was something different about the man to whom I directed the question. His t-shirt was less worn, perhaps, his manner one of authority. Sure enough, he was "The General" in person. Hamed gets things done. He is the contractor, the broker, the man in charge, the fixer. The man to order things from, to arrange things with. When the film company was shooting *Mountains of the Moon,* using Lamu for the Zanzibar sequence, it was Hamed who came up with the extras, all of them. "I fitted them out for their costumes, I supplied their props." Maybe he was exaggerating but never mind.

He not only arranged to have us returned forthwith to the hotel but suggested we refresh ourselves with a sundown cruise through the mangrove swamp. He would personally accompany us. We immediately accepted. If camel caravans crossed the northern route, it was the dhows that sailed the southern trade lanes, the boats, and their sailors, that changed the course of maritime history, when Rome refused to pay Parthian tariffs and by the second century had opened new markets, and new routes south through the Red Sea and across the Indian Ocean, testing navigational instruments, and running cargoes of ivory, slaves, spices, gold and silk.

After the high tide cruise and a spectacular equatorial sunset we returned to Peponi's for a cup of tea on the veranda, then a superb dinner of "rainbow runner". The sky is blistered with constellations, confused by the latitude, out of order and at random, but crowded and bright. We sleep to the lullaby of an overhead fan in the double mosquito netting, the breeze in the palm fronds and the breathy stillness of the soft air.

WEDNESDAY, NOVEMBER 1

I had told Hamed I wanted to walk on the beach. He laughed and said I would have all the beach in the world. Tomás protested. He had gone out early to swim before the sun came up and found the sand soft, unpleasant for walking and very tiring. Hamed laughed again. "You have to wait for the tide to go out." Tomás insisted but Hamed dismissed him with a wave of his sun-darkened hand. He told me, "walk all the way around the island if you want, about twelve and a half kilometers on each side, roughly thirty-eight kilometers in all. Is that enough of a walk for you?"

When he saw my blank look he relented a little. "OK, from Peponi's to the point is about twelve kilometers. It may not sound like much but the sand is hard as asphalt when the tide goes out, the sun is very hot, and there is nothing between here and there, so be warned."

We started out with no particular intention of walking from one spot to another. We were just going to the beach. The tide, in effect, far out in the late morning, had uncovered a vast expanse of sand, and a bright sun reflecting off the water. After so many days on game drives, and no exercise, it seemed tantalizing, irresistible, but just for a stroll. After all, at home, back then, I easily jogged ten kilometers a day, but I never counted, or kept a record. It was just a guess.

So I just threw a flowing robe over my bathing suit, wrapped a *pareu* around my waist, and following the example of the bearers on the wharf, a neckerchief. And a white terrycloth turban, and over that a visor, that I grabbed as an afterthought, to shade my eyes. It said "Acapulco" and I was sure it would impress the locals. If they had never heard of Mexico, why would they have heard of Acapulco? But I wasn't thinking. I even left my marvelous walking shoes in the room, just took a pair of flip-flops down to the shore. I would regret this, bitterly.

Maybe I was still yearning for the Masai Mara, maybe I still envisioned the "endless plain" as something that belonged to me, I was perhaps bewitched by Kenya's vast spaces. At first we just splashed in the tide pools, beside a line of dunes that stretched, as if an engineer had designed them with a slide rule, in what seemed a straight line to a point clearly visible just up the beach. I left Tomás looking at the minute inhabitants of the little screw shells on the sand, entrusted my towel and flip-flops to him, and remarked casually that I was just going for a stroll.

"Don't go too far," he replied, assuming a severe tone. "The sun is very strong."

I could see how white my legs were and how long it had been since I had done any serious sunbathing, or in fact, even been exposed to the elements. "I should have asked Tomás for his sun block," I thought to myself. "I'll use it when I get back. I'm only going to that point up there. Should be a couple of kilometers."

And so I set out, perversely knowing I had every intention of going the full twelve kilometers. The endless beach was exhilarating, my adrenaline was up, and I was enveloped by euphoria; I could walk forever. I hit my stride and wanted never to stop.

Soon the last stragglers among the sun worshippers were gone. The Danish couple who owned Peponi's, throwing a ball for their German shepherd, were far behind me. There were no birds, no people, no boats, not even a stray donkey, and the reef had gone off in another direction. The point, just beyond the touch of my fingertips, remained at the same distance as when I had started. I was making no advancement at all. The sun was higher in the sky. My feet began to blister. I started jogging, striking the hard sand with my heel, to change my balance.

Twelve kilometers up is also twelve kilometers back. I thought of turning around. My skin was burning, even under my clothes. I walked closer to the water's edge to cool my feet. Then I realized the sun on the water was like a magnifying glass, burning holes in my legs. At first I didn't feel a thing, and still I continued. How could I give up if I had come this far? Did Stanley turn back? Did Livingstone? On the other hand, Napoleon turned back because he knew he was defeated. Gordon anticipated his own death to prove a point but he was driven to it. And if I died, out here on this empty beach, it would take someone longer to find the body than to return it for disposal.

And still the point evaded me. I almost felt shipwrecked and began to search for signs of land on the sea of sand, with no beginning or end. The vibrant equatorial air was playing its tricks. And the stubborn determination to triumph. Triumph over what? Suddenly I realized how foolish I was behaving, how much I was compromising Tomás or my children if anything happened to me. And so, with the point and its mystery just ahead I turned back; and felt wiser for the choice.

The walk back was long and while I still felt elated, I was in pain from the blisters on the bottoms of my feet. I was leaving bloody tracks in the sand. I could admit that now. I had taken no water but still had no sensation of thirst. I started talking to myself, or singing, or reciting any poetry I could remember. It was a long time, at a trot, before I saw any sunbathers, or the playful dog, or the blonde girl with her black lover from the sailing yacht anchored off Peponi's. Then I saw something strange. A small cotton tent, with a very red leg hanging out of it. The leg was partially covered by a beach towel. It was Tomás, waiting for me. He had found a stick of mangrove and was holding it aloft, like a tent pole, to fashion a shelter out of his own *pareu,* his towel protecting his legs as much as possible. He was bright red, his blue eyes like limpid pools reflecting the sea, but red rimmed and swollen. I felt so sorry for him I forgot my own burns and wanted to kneel beside him, or embrace him or cover him with kisses but it would have hurt both of us too much.

We stumbled to our feet and headed for the hotel, ignoring the hippies on the terrace, the honeymoon couple from Canada that had caught up with us, the startled tourists who had just arrived. "Lunch is nearly over," said Agatha, the English girl who managed the kitchen, "but I saved some yellow-tail for you. Want some water?"

It was all we could do to make it to the shower, letting the cool water rehydrate the scalded flesh, then dry off under the overhead fan. The touch of a towel was too painful. We slathered each other with "cancer guard" and drank more water. "Hamed is coming for us at three o'clock to sail up to the ruins of Takwa," said Tomás, almost accusingly. I said I would be ready.

I carefully covered all my skin with long cotton pants, long socks and a long-sleeved shirt, then added the turban and the Acapulco visor, which at least had complemented my sun glasses to keep the glare off my face. The dhow came for us but Hamed had other things to do. He had sent Isaac, the boatman, and his own cousin Alí—half black and half Arab—in a ragged t-shirt, torn shorts and a nearly toothless smile, but eyes that were soft and loving, and a kind, furrowed face.

13.

ISAAC THE BOATMAN ON A LOCAL DHOW

We entered the mangroves but the tide was not fully in. As we approached Takwa, with its fourteenth century ruins, all that remains of a community of twenty-five hundred people, a beautiful young boy in a *khanga* or sarong, a boatman out of Paradise, came up with his dugout canoe to help us over the coral and red clay. His happy smile and clear, bright eyes disguised the fact that his speech was impaired: he was brain damaged. And so he became the cherub of the Styx, a deceptive Charon in the equatorial swamp, to me, an angel, for I had to remove my shoes and socks, roll up the white trousers and reveal the red flesh and the bleeding blisters. No mind, I thought. Where I come from the sun no longer burns after three in the afternoon. But this is not where I come from.

Everywhere about us were tombs, mosques, homes and stores, all in mournful ruin, tumbled and overgrown, where now the birds and the monkeys frolic in the thorn bushes and the shady pines and coconuts. Salt water filtered into the wells and the people moved to Shella, only to have to leave again, many years later. "Elephants once wandered through these woods," says Alí, "but they are long gone." He lends me a hand to scramble down the sand and red clay path, lined with scrub growth, and over the dunes to the water's edge, where the beach is carpeted with little crabs. We laugh. "You won't walk here," says Alí. Ah, so the story of my misadventures has spread.

14.

RUINS OF A MOSQUE IN FOURTEENTH CENTURY TAKWA

A caretaker dispatches us at the entrance to the ruins, now a national monument, and sends us back to our Charon. The dhow pulls into the mangrove web, among yellow butterflies and bright birds, where a luxuriant sunset in a striated sky sends us along on the whisper of the wind, back across the channel to Peponi's.

Dinner, of amberjack in ginger sauce, is a delight. I had missed my lunch but I had seen the Portals of the Universe face to face, or so I thought. We ran into Alí on the terrace. He was immaculately dressed in a new shirt and clean *khanga,* his hair combed and slicked down. "What happened, Alí? I hardly recognize you."

"Evening prayers," he mutters. "For God, one' best."

THURSDAY, NOVEMBER 2

We sail along the channel back to town, where the Lamu Express drops off the local passengers before crossing to Manda and the broken pier. We tiptoe along the barnacle-encrusted supports, sliding and slipping, especially in my currently crippled state, while I clutch the Australian Outback hat which is all that stands between me and a bash on the head.

A Cessna 404 is waiting, with a black Kenyan pilot and co-pilot. A jaunty sign in clumsy, childlike writing, bids us a jovial farewell: *Karibu* ("You are welcome"), *Kwaheri ya kuonana* ("Hope you had a good stay"). And so for the *wanaosafari* or "departure", ten minutes due north, as we bank around the edge of the island over tidepools and mangroves, leaving behind Takwa and the long beach on Lamu.

We come in quickly, over the clay houses and thatched roofs of a fishing village, just to one side of a perfect, horseshoe bay, completely contained within a reef and corked by a coral island, with a Morse-code coastline both north and south: dots and dashes of sand, coral and brush. The plane banks sharply over the beach and palm-scrub dunes, then turns left one hundred and eighty degrees onto the grass landing strip. The pilot brought his own porter from Lamu. The boy fetches our bags from the hold, deposits them on the landing strip, collects the bags of the departing passengers and turns to reboard without a word.

A sign verifies that we have arrived at the Kiwayu Safari Village but the plane takes off and leaves us standing, surrounded by our belongings, in the middle of a deserted grass clearing, near a hut that passes for a waiting room. Then we hear a vehicle, veering along a sand track that serves as a road. The boys from the hotel get out and with a certain flourish, place a wooden footstool, with four steps, by the side of the Land Rover, to assist our ascent, especially mine, since unbeknownst to them, I can hardly walk.

They drive us to a collection of grass and thatch huts with grass mat floors, open on all sides. The desk clerk checks us in but we are told the rooms have yet to be made up. He invites us, meantime, to refreshments in the main hut—the lounge and dining room— a glass of Evian water, very acceptable. The hut's floors and walls are all grass mats. Palm trees grow in the middle, up through the thatched roof. Tables are waxed wooden beams of different shapes and sizes with simple slat benches, piled high with outsized cushions, all covered in colorful Kenya cotton, without repeating a single design. Each length of cloth has a legend woven into it, sayings and bits of wisdom from the popular culture, in Swahili.

The Italian architect and designer who built Kiwayu fourteen years earlier had a unique and unerring taste for the *objet trouvé,* a notion then much in fashion. All the decoration, inside and out, was natural: elephant skulls, whale vertebrae, monkey bones, glass fishing floats, shells, driftwood, pods from the scrubland, thorny dead branches. The long bar was made of local rattan.

The owners were French and the hotel had been run, for the past four and a half years, by a Parisian, assisted by a French chef. Bread baskets were lined with quilted cozies. The coaster for my water glass had been woven from grass matting. Lettuce is brought from Nairobi each Wednesday and salad is formally served, as in a Paris *bistro.* Meals are usually prepared from the morning's fishing, brought from the village at the end of the bay: tuna, *kolikoli,* dolphin (*dorado* or mahi-mahi), sailfish and an occasional marlin or shark from deep water, but lobster is also prevalent, and marvelous. Agatha, the girl from the kitchen at Peponi's, had already alerted us, when we debated her menu, not to waste our time with Lamu lobster, as we would have plenty, and better, in Kiwayu. "Take advantage of my fish and sauces." She was absolutely right.

The hours in Kiwayu are flexible. Breakfast is served all morning. People drag in off the beach for lunch nearly at sundown. Dinner is served as late as desired and is followed by a cheese table and dessert buffet, then coffee or tea in the lounge.

The shop is equally unscheduled. If it happens to be open there are useful things, like suntan lotion, an interesting selection of books in several languages, cotton cloth of the sort used on the cushions, wooden beads and native jewelry. The girl in charge was intrigued by the fact that we came from a place about which she knew nothing. The visor from Acapulco caught her eye. She had friends everywhere in Europe, she said, so we explained her problem. She knew no one from the American continent. "Someday," she went on, "I will meet a friend who will take me from here to another place, maybe even to Europe, but I'm sure it will not be to Mexico. I don't know where it is."

Tomás bought four lengths of heavy white cotton from her, to be used for *khangas*, shawls or *pareus*. She spent hours twisting the ends and knotting them for us, making a handsome fringe.

Three English boys, blond, sunburned, eighteen and enthusiastic, present themselves and by way of introduction offer their services as snorkeling or wind surfing instructors, or as guides for a fishing trip out to the reef. I explain that I am out of commission so instead we talk. They ask us what they should buy that could later be converted to cash, since they are unable to export their Kenyan earnings. We suggest the exotic jewelry of the tribes, or perhaps woven cloth, especially from Somalia, which is only thirty-five kilometers north of here. Sea shells, coral and marine life are out, as they are on the endangered list all over the world.

We are joined by the manager, who seems sympathetic about my burns. He produces a tube of zinc oxide ointment, a Yugoslavian formula, manufactured in Kenya. "It's all I have," he says, by way of apology, "but ice will also help." The boys, with Celtic skin like Tomás', very pale, with blue eyes, had all suffered burns and reburns and more burns again. Their noses and shoulders were peeling and one boy's chin was in dire condition. They all claimed, however, that the ointment, though long ago expired, had been very helpful.

The little bay is a voluptuous, sloping line embraced by low brush and grass. The hotel is nestled in a coconut oasis in the very center. Petrol drums are being unloaded on the beach for fuel. Water, though very scarce, is obtained from deep wells and guests are advised to make the best possible use of it.

♫♫♫

Our rooms are finally ready. We had the good fortune, or the manager saw fit, to assign us number ten of the seventy huts available, the closest to the restaurant, which facilitated my limited mobility. It was really a little house, worthy of Gauguin at Hiva Oa. The large living room had both a wooden base, piled high with huge cushions, and a hammock facing an aperture, devoid of glass but equipped with a grass mat panel on a cord, to be rolled up or down at will, looking out on the secluded coconut grove and the sea. The box which served as a coffee table was covered with grass mats by way of upholstery. Floors and walls were also grass mats. Another window looked into the bedroom, which is entered by a doorway equally protected by a grass mat panel, rolled up and tied during the day. A hall in front of the bedroom is furnished with two wooden chairs with a wooden table between them, for the contemplation of the scenery during early morning tea.

The hall and bedroom are decorated with yellow cotton curtains, turquoise bedspread and chair cushions. The bedroom is very large, with a king sized bed consisting of a foam rubber mattress on a wooden frame. The headboard is upholstered with grass mat. A turquoise cotton canopy not only supports the veil of the mosquito netting—the first we had found that was really clean—but keeps the frolicking sand crabs from dancing off the closet roof onto the sleeping guest during the night, when they take their flying leaps into the silent darkness.

A reed sofa and chairs with coffee table, in one corner of the bedroom, whose cushions are also turquoise cotton with yellow-tasseled trim, turn the area into a sitting room. A basket on the table, decorated with red yarn, contains a complete dressmaker's sewing kit. A Thermos holds drinking water.

The dressing room, with access from either side of the bedroom, is reached through doors with grass mat panels. The rack—for the yellow and turquoise color-coordinated towels—is a dead tree held in place on a driftwood beam. There is no charge for laundry, which is collected in a large hamper, woven of palm. The double sinks are set into a dressing table, with ample counter space, accompanied by two stools, one for each side, and a long mirror. A double closet made of grass matting serves as the division between the sleeping and the dressing areas, as well as the nocturnal playground for the sand crabs. At night there is electricity but during the day the lighting comes in through the open space running along the full length between the grass mat walls and the beams that support the thatched roof. The coconuts flutter in the private, sandy garden all around this enchanted miniature kingdom and beyond them, a pale blue sky lurks behind scuttling clouds.

Two doors lead off the dressing area. One is the ample grass-and-mat stall shower, with a wooden slat rack over the sand on the ground. A wooden shelf holds shampoo, soap, wash cloth, whatever. The other door leads to a clothesline in a grass mat service hallway, open to the sky and very handy for towels or wet bathing suits, and contains as well a spacious grass mat cubicle for a standard flush toilet. The holder for the roll of toilet paper is a hemp rope strung diagonally across a corner.

There might be many such hotels or resort villages in the world today, but in 1989 this was Paradise, and a model for an ecstatic hideaway in a natural setting, greatly imaginative and elegant, with exemplary handling of proportion and space. Good taste is a talent, born, not taught, unaffected by the price of its component elements.

FRIDAY, NOVEMBER 3

The incapacitated, temporarily or otherwise, have two choices: complain or adapt. I suppose if someone else is to blame there is a certain amount of accusation or denial involved: "I am only an innocent victim", "This didn't really happen" or "Why me?"

Since I had willfully provoked my own infirmity none of these applied. I had second-degree burns and was in the middle of the Indian Ocean coast of Africa, with nothing available but an expired zinc oxide ointment and ice packs, analgesics in case of pain—of which there was practically none—and an antibiotic cream to ward off infection, actually the greatest danger, but it helped not at all and only served to inflame the burns. I was beginning to blister.

In the idyllic surroundings of Kiwayu there was little difficulty in reconciling desires and appetites with my tangible possibilities. There could be no thought of walking on the beach, exploring the fishing village, swimming the channel to the coral isle or snorkeling on the reef. I was therefore free to do something unusual, and for me, unheard of. Nothing.

So I delivered myself, in the greatest spirit of total peace, to the enjoyment of my grass house and discovered the Paradise within. The soft lullaby of the water in the baylet, the driftwood and the shells, baskets and cotton and phrases of native wisdom, became the open spaces that are not empty and I was unspeakably happy.

My next project turned into a survey of the Swahili phrases on the cushions in my room and in the lounge. With the help of the barman, waiters, and the girl from the shop, we approximated the following translations:

"Sea Creature: six legs and a shell". I knew what that was. I had seen the tiny tracks on the sandy floor of the shower.

"A poor man's home is always noisy".

"A wise leader keeps peace among his people".

"One tree trunk is different from any other".

"The heart is not a book, it reads differently".
"Never favor the ungrateful".
"Do not favor who is not shy". Referring here to "modest".
"Money means a good job".

SATURDAY, NOVEMBER 4

A quiet morning reading, studying coastal lore and Swahil history. The swelling is bad and the blisters are monstrous, some of them are broken and draining, others just burgeoning like balloons, all over my legs. Trying to lie still and keep my legs on the ice packs.

Fresh lobster for lunch (Agatha was right), with *ratatouille,* miniature pizzas, fresh Brussels' sprouts, salad with fresh greens, fruit and cheese, followed by tea in the lounge. The plane has radioed its approach so we dress to leave for the airfield. I keep my clothes, especially the socks, as clean as possible. As we check out I see the girl from the shop by the desk. She has two chums with her. She drops her gaze as I pass, until on an impulse I tear off the visor from Acapulco and hand it to her. Her face lights up. As soon as I turn my back she is jumping up and down, her arms round her friends' shoulders.

Another honeymoon couple, this one from England, under the thatched lean-to that passes for a waiting room facing the landing strip. Turns out he is a medical student from London. He asks to photograph my blisters. "Never seen anything like this."

The Cessna arrives and we take off over the Tana River country, the primate reserve and green woods which an hour later become the arid plains around Nairobi, a little greener now, with the rains.

After checking back into the Nairobi Safari Club and claiming our bags from storage Tomás goes out to find an apothecary. The word "drugstore" does not apply in Kenya. He comes back much later, with hydrogen peroxide for disinfecting the draining wounds and plenty of gauze bandages. "It took longer than I thought because

I had to choose the bandages that were still sealed from the laboratory. The boy at the counter offered me all sorts of shapes and sizes but when I asked him how he knew what they were he said, "because I opened them to see…".

He had also brought a hypodermic needle, to draw off the liquid from the larger blisters, that were still growing. He was afraid that if he waited until they burst half the skin on my legs would be lifted off the flesh, increasing the danger of infection and taking longer to heal. There were twenty-five milliliters of liquid in each blister, in addition to the water that dripped through the hole made by the needle, and this drained all night. No wonder I was always thirsty.

SUNDAY, NOVEMBER 5

It was the most beautiful day I had seen in Nairobi, with clear skies and dazzling sun. After breakfast, however, which I had sent to the room, while Tomás went back to the shops for his stones and beads, I stayed quietly in my room, flat on my back in bed, reading Beryl Markham with my feet up on ice packs. I suppose this is the difference between "being" as opposed to "doing".

In the afternoon, after Tomás treated my burns, I was allowed to go down to the lounge, to have tea with the Mexican Ambassador and his wife. We made arrangements to have dinner at Tamarind on our return from Zimbabwe, to which we departed the next day.

MONDAY, NOVEMBER 6

The morning is overcast and grim. We run a few last-minute errands before leaving for the airport. My burns are better but still bandaged. The bottoms of my feet are also better but very swollen, and I walk with a severe limp. My wonderful shoes have grown mis-shapen and crooked. The burned skin is about to peel.

The sky clears in the early afternoon but our flight is delayed. We have spent the last of our Kenyan shillings and kept dollars aside for the airport departure tax, what seemed then to be an exorbitant twenty U.S. dollars per passenger. This keeps nationals, I suppose, within their own boundaries and on the ground.

We are finally called to our flight on Air Zimbabwe's Boeing 737. This southern Africa's prestige airline, with its British pilot, takes us on a five hour flight, first across Tanzania, then down the very elongated vertical sliver of Lake Malawi, which like everything else in Africa, seems smaller on the map than it really is. Originally Lake Nyasa or Niassa, in what is now Mozambique, formerly Nyasaland, this third largest and second deepest is the southernmost of the lakes in the East African Rift system. It is also the ninth largest lake in the world, reportedly the habitat of more species of fish than any other body of fresh water on earth, including over one thousand species of *cichlids,* in 1911 declared a national reserve.

We cross arid plains with their clusters of huts, strewn about a ruddy, rust-red landscape, and finally approach the neat and fertile farmland, the gracious homes with orderly gardens and swimming pools and the carefully laid out factories in the industrial areas around Zimbabwe's capital Harare, formerly Salisbury.

Zimbabwe, previously Southern Rhodesia—named for Cecil John Rhodes, an English entrepreneur and mining magnate, head of DeBeers, and a political adventurer who claimed the territory in 1887—was then a very prosperous country of ten million, with a racial proportion of about ten blacks to every white. It had gained its independence only ten years earlier. The strong ruling party, under black nationalist Robert Mugabe, had initially supported the then-prevalent policy of "to govern is to populate", but he reversed himself, as most modern leaders did, when he realized what a strain he was putting on his available resources.

Today Zimbabwe is a disaster, Mugabe continues in power and nothing went according to plan, but in 1989 currency was stable at two Zim-dollars to one U.S. dollar, with a twenty percent inflation. The country's economy was determined by its alliance with the European Economic Community, to which it exported wheat, soybeans, maize, beef, even flowers, as well as most of its tobacco. The tobacco auction house was reputed to have been the second largest in the world. A fledgling wine industry was at that time also evolving into an important potential export. Farming and production, back then, were concentrated largely in the hands of third and fourth generation Zimbabweans, of European parentage, who considered the country as much or more their own as did the blacks, to whom they referred disparagingly as "africans" or worse, yet after Independence it was the "africans" who administered the political and economic structure and who obliged repatriation of all foreign exchange, to the consternation of the whites.

The whites discounted the blacks, as far as they were concerned ill qualified either to till or to govern, lacking in any heritage of art or cultural history, though no one can explain Great Zimbabwe, from which the new land took its name. This remarkable stone city to the south, built over a period of three centuries, from the ninth to the eleventh, with its mighty perimeter walls, conical towers, its acropolis, its enclosure, along with other structures now in total ruin, may have been, as the whites claim, an Arab stronghold—a fortress or trading post—built by native labor. Blacks, however, in the name of national identity, or perhaps plain logic, assure us that this is unlikely, if not impossible, so far inland and so distant— and so far south—of the known Arab trade lanes; and consider it more likely the work of Africans, upper case, whose knowledge, civilization and cultural achievements have always been minimized—eroded or profaned—by centuries of "perverse and sadistic European domination".

TUESDAY, NOVEMBER 7

Our gilded, box-shaped Sheraton Hotel, Health Club and Convention Center, outside the center of town and known to the locals as "Benson & Hedges", were extravagantly modern, designed according to international formula with a certain veneer of Miami or Las Vegas. The broad and lively lobby included a noisy bar, as well as other more sedate bars and restaurants, that competed with the traditional places downtown. The shops offered gem-stones, native as well as contemporary sculpture carved in a green onyx known as *verdite,* and unlimited ivory and animal skins, the former badly carved and the latter badly cured. The government's official line encouraged the legal "culling" of the elephant herds to the extent of three thousand head per year, "because elephants are a menace to villages and farms and reproduce too copiously to guarantee an adequate food supply". The elephants are only reasonably safe, then, in certain game parks and we were able to gain information as to only two leopards in the entire country, in a cage at the Crocodile Farm, which doubles as a modest feline zoo, at Victoria Falls.

The view from the window of our hotel room, looking out across the sprawling suburbs and one residential neighborhood after another, revealed more than anything else the cinnabar-red countryside, brick-tiled rooftops and exuberant flame trees in full bloom, against a background of green woods and bright sky. The best view, however, was just nearby, overlooking the skyline from the *kopje,* Harare's highest point, where the first British settlers raised the Union Jack. The "native" quarter spills around the base of the rock formation, with its lively shops, heady aromas and bus-tling market, but we were asked politely not to go there unescorted.

We set out after breakfast, ignoring the shuttle bus to town, and limped through the hotel grounds and beyond, to the new ZANU ruling party headquarters, in construction at the corner. Former offices had been blown up by the opposition. Traffic was heavy but hardly prohibitive, since the import both of cars and spare parts was strictly forbidden, except with a costly permit, hard to come by, but a privilege that could be sold after two years.

Zimbabwe is distinguished by two major cultural groups, the Shona in this part of the country and principal authors of the verdite sculpture we had seen; and the Matabele, which we were to encounter later, near the western border. No Swahili is spoken here and we miss the jaunty *"Jambo!"* everywhere we go. People are handsome but less stylized in their beauty. The task of most hairdressers here, more than in East Africa, is the straightening or the bleaching of hair. We saw fewer braids but far more school note-books. An important university was closed by government troops in response to student demands, not unlike other parts of the world at that time, but education was hard won: books and study materi-als, laboratory artifacts, art supplies, were scarce and expensive. We found a few second hand bookshops and libraries, but literacy among blacks, either in English or Africaans, the two colonial *lingua franca,* was very limited.

The whites, on the other hand, had their garden clubs, their quilting bees or cake-bakes, and their luncheons at the pavilion in the park where lower class blacks could only sprawl on the grass at lunchtime. This privileged ten percent held charity events and bazaars and ran swap shops and garage sales, to support the Orphaned Animals' Home or the Horse Sanctuary ("for ill or mis-treated horses").

Since the "Chicken Run" during the uprisings more than a decade earlier, when about eighty thousand settlers fled, the Zimbabweans who remained became more visibly nationalistic, completely com-mitted to the country and determined to hold on unless somehow forced to leave. The émigrés, however, still came back for holidays, to visit the relatives who remained behind and to spend the money they were unable to take out of the country, when they moved to Australia, South Africa or Botswana. When people live in a single place, or function within an established orbit, their symbols remain fairly static, with a very limited margin for opinion or dialogue. And so it was in Zimbabwe, with those who stayed or those who left. They saw no injustice or imbalance, no pillage of nature or waste; and their lives, their schools and churches, the structure of their leisure or their orientation in public service, the department stores and pedestrian streets, shopping centers and sidewalk cafés, gave Harare, once insular Salisbury, an air of a provincial city in Europe or the United States. For as long as it lasted, it was a good life, over-flowing with rustic heartiness.

We were still able to sample a bit of it in the Modern Art Museum downtown, near the Monomatapa Hotel on Julius Nyerere Avenue, facing the park. In fact, the sculpture garden opened directly onto the park, so enjoyed an especially spacious and carefully groomed background. The museum was supported by citizen and church groups who awarded prizes to encourage both blacks and whites to express an aesthetic language rooted in their cultural heritage. Wood, stone and ceramic, with some "soft" sculpture in cloth or synthetics, seemed to be looking for a unique and personal idiom and the pieces we saw, in an exhibit devoted to "Zimbabwe Heritage", offered a wide variety and degree of accomplishment. The alternatives, evident in the shop in our hotel, where Shona sculptors had been trained by Italian marble carvers, were flimsy and fictitious.

In the Queen Victoria Museum, on the other hand, we found everything from art and history to paleontology and the natural sciences. Probably the most interesting displays had to do with the Bushmen cave paintings, little known except through the books of Laurens van der Post or the film *The Gods Must Be Crazy* (Jamie Uys, 1980).

The diminutive brown Bushmen, with the bland features and tightly curled hair, were an indigenous people, astonishingly resourceful in the arts of survival, whose territory spanned most of South Africa, Zimbabwe, Lesotho, Mozambique, Swaziland, Botswana, Namibia and Angola. They were also described as San, Sho, Basarwa, Kung or Khwe, but essentially belong to the hunter-gatherer Khoisan group, which includes the pastoral Khoikhoi. They were, in effect, the first known inhabitants of the region, as revealed in their cave and rock paintings all over Southern Africa, noteworthy aesthetically because they never illustrated an event, as such, but rather translated the spirit or sensation of the experience, perhaps the truest definition of abstract art.

⸱ They were nevertheless hunted for sport by the early European farmers and settlers, who claimed a bounty for their trophies; and they survive only in Botswana, where the largest extension of the Kalahari Desert, the only home that remains to them, can be found.

♪♪♪

Zimbabwe included enormous coal deposits and under the right circumstances it might have served for synthetic fuel. Unfortunately the formula was developed by the Germans during the Second World War and has been controlled by the British, as part of the arrangements for surrender. Fuel in 1989 was imported from South Africa and reduced with ethanol. It smelled terrible and in addition to my limp, made walking around Harare less than pleasant.

Water, on the other hand, abounded, and artesian wells maintained, among other luxuries, no fewer than twenty-nine golf courses, to satisfy the restrictions of the various sectors. Schools were nonetheless integrated by law. Offices nominally offered equal opportunities, by race and sex. Servants were nevertheless invariably black. The whites tended to own and run their own shops, especially in excursion and other clothing, and much of this was manufactured in the country, along with animal products, furniture, appliances, office supplies and high level professional services. "We live together," we are told, "but our cultures are very different."

Our source maintains that he would have no objection to his daughter, age four, bringing home black playmates from school, "but if she did the same thing at age eighteen her mother and I would be horrified."

WEDNESDAY, NOVEMBER 8

We are up before dawn. The chill wind is deceptive. By midday the heat will be suffocating. The skies are clear as we depart for Victoria Falls on another Air Zimbabwe 737, among many Australian tourists; and a charming black couple from the States traveling with their three small children, as well as the wife's mother and father, whose parents were born in Zimbabwe. The whole family plans to move back to Harare. We ran into them all over the country and became rather friendly and later remained in contact by way of the letters we wrote, sealed in airmail envelopes with tricolor borders, the way it used to be. The wife had been on radio and TV in Los Angeles and her husband was a producer of television films, looking to get into communications in Southern Africa.

We were also accompanied by an Indian shopkeeper with his wife and young son, vacationing from Nairobi, very enthused by our obvious delight with Kenya.

Then there was the disquieting young couple from New Zealand. He was very ill, with chills and fever. We guessed he was suffering from a malaria attack, so offered aspirin but there was nothing more we could do.

The entire landscape below us was divided into neat and orderly parcels. The "Zimbabwean" farmers feel threatened by the "africans" and the problem, as we see it, is just as much cultural as racial. Before the land is cleared it looks clipped and wooly, like the black heads under their maze of infinitesimal braids, and produces modestly, to satisfy the needs of small groups of people. Under the extensive cultivation strategies of the whites, however, while the bright red soil initially yields generous crops of grains, pasturage, fruit and vegetables, it has to be nurtured. It is easily depleted.

♫♫♫

The locals at "Vic Falls" consider their runway to be the longest in the world. Which of course it is not. Yet for some reason planes find it difficult getting off the ground in the dense, cloying heat. One enterprising company even tried to establish an excursion service, with hydroplanes on the Zambezi River, but the planes never got into the air.

Airports in Zimbabwe are conventional affairs. None of the makeshift, offhand landing strips of Kenya. We have passenger terminals, control towers, military installations in close vigilance nearby and warnings against photography, not really vigorously enforced.

The tarmacs were carved from the woodland of even, low trees, scrub growth and red soil, in a setting that is essentially flat and homogeneous, except that the huge waves of mist thrown up by the great river create a legitimate rain forest within its banks. The Zambezi is, in fact, a tributary of the Congo River System emerging from Lake Tanganyika in Central Equatorial Africa. Livingstone verified that it flows eastward from what is now Angola, drains the border with Zambia, then crosses Mozambique before emptying into the Indian Ocean, between Sofala and Quelimane. How could the good doctor have mistaken this for the source of the Nile?

We are met by an A&K van driven by blonde and blue-eyed Tracy, sturdy and wholesome, and like most of the Zimbabwean women we had met she was also a good driver, with a steady gaze, very much at ease and eager to find a way to travel abroad—not very likely with currency restrictions. She wore the company uniform but with sandals, in the manner of a wild little country girl accustomed to going barefoot.

She gave us a tour on our way into the village, a look at the local cattle and remarked especially on the dung beetle, one of the ecological mainstays of Southern Africa, "guided and oriented," she tells us, "by the Milky Way."

"A scarab!" we cry, delighted with our own perception and perspicacity, but she was nonplussed. "A what?" She had never heard the term before, nor had any idea of its importance in ancient Egypt, where it was deified. The messengers of the gods were patent in even the lowliest of creatures.

She had stopped us cold, nevertheless, and was one up on The Milky Way. It was many years before an article appeared in National Geographic, ("Weird and Wild", January 24, 2013), to verify what was apparently common knowledge in Southern Africa, and unique in the animal kingdom.

Tracy still had to get even for the *scarab*, however, so stopped by a large *baobab* tree. "This was used by Dr. David Livingstone as his headquarters during his stay near the falls. He was transported in a canoe by the local Makalolo people to the very edge of the precipice, and he was much impressed."

∫∫∫

We check into the Makasa Sun Hotel and Casino, in the village, not really a town at all, just a few shops and offices, a bank and a railroad stop, with a larger hotel, the Victoria Falls, overlooking the bridge into Zambia.

We start out for the falls, one of the great cataracts of the world, through a festival of outrageous aromas: the heat rising in waves from the harsh grass underfoot, tinged with the scent of sweat, and this somehow merges with the musky shade of the woods, the soaked grass behind the hotel, the sweet scent of a newly-mowed lawn. We startle a bushbuck, an alert little female. Her mate, proud and aloof, stands panting a short distance away.

This is the low water season, Tracy tells us, "happily for you." Normally the water, wedged into an abyss—an abrupt slash across the landscape—crashes with such force that the cataracts themselves are impossible to see. At its peak this is the widest sheet of falling water in the world, seventeen hundred meters across and approximately one hundred meters deep into the bowels of the canyon, one and one half times wider than Niagara and twice its height.

Livingstone, the first known European to see the falls in November of 1855, as he explored the twenty-seven hundred kilometers of the Zambezi River, named them in honor of Queen Victoria, for whom Lake Victoria was also named. This lent itself to no small confusion. Actually, the falls that emerge from Lake Victoria, into Lake Albert, were named for George Frederick Samual Robinson, the Marquis of Ripon. They correspond to another river, in another country, flowing in another direction.

$$\text{\emph{ʃʃʃ}}$$

The greatest known flow of water over Victoria Falls, launching spray high into the air and obliterating the countryside as far as the eye can see, was over seven hundred thousand cubic meters per minute. Normally the flow varies from five hundred to fifty thousand in the peak season, to an average of twenty thousand in the slack.

A lunar rainbow, a local phenomenon, occurs when a brave full moon, like the one now growing in the evening sky, falls on the mist and vapor thrust by the falls into the silvery night. Special arrangements can be made with park authorities for viewing the lunar rainbow. For regular daytime admission non-Zimbabweans at that time paid one Zim-dollar entrance fee. Zimbabweans, however, were required to produce an identity card, a subtle way of checking on the migration through a tourist region, with refugees and renegades scattering at this corner where Botswana, Zambia and Zimbabwe come together and where contraband is rampant.

The falls were presumably formed about one hundred and fifty million years ago, during the Jurassic Period, of heightened volcanic activity and massive eruptions, which left a thick layer of lava covering the earth's surface. As the basalt cooled it began to shrink, thus opening fissures which later, as a result of erosion, coupled with seismic activity, grew wider, until five essential cataracts were formed here: "The Devil's Cataract", "Main Falls", "Horseshoe Falls", "Rainbow Falls" and the "Eastern Cataract" on the Zambian side.

Paleolithic tools found in surface deposits of sand and gravel attest to the presence of stone age man along the river's banks, and indicate that it has taken the Zambezi over ten thousand years to sculpt its course in its present form, though the chasm is always remodeled, every season. Victoria, however, is only one—though considered the greatest—of many waterfalls found along the course of the rivers on the ancient plateau in the southern cone of the continent.

This "greatest known curtain of falling water" was called *Mosi oa Tunya,* "The Smoke That Thunders". To Livingstone it had seemed a spectacle worthy of "halting angels in their flight". And so a light aircraft takes visitors on a fifteen minute tour over the falls and calls it "The Flight of Angels". The brilliant blooms called "Blood Lilies" or "pin cushion flowers" peer through the rain forest at the base of the chasm and dot the green walls with their crimson fluff, but they are not foolish: they know the difference between rain and spray. They only bloom during the rainy season.

There have been a number of attempts to capitalize on the falls for recreational purposes. One company tried the hydroplane scheme, which was abandoned. Another thought hot air ballooning a good idea but it was too dangerous and was also discarded. Speed boats take passengers upriver from the falls, especially for sundown tea or Zimbabwean champagne, in the groves on the islets in the middle of the river, amid clouds of butterflies, almost as dense as the mist itself. During low water there is no lack of adrenaline junkies who curl up in the puddles on the rim of the precipice, to tempt fate and gravity. Rafting is the one sport deemed feasible down the canyon below the cataracts and in fact we ran into a camera crew following a team down into the gorge on the Zambian side, where it is easier to reach the water's edge. The whole idea was to savor some of the river's wild power and demonic speed before it came to be trapped and tamed in Lake Kariba, which we will discover later in our journey.

Wildlife is certainly not the attraction. Other than birds and monkeys, and a few waterbuck, there are few animals. The local prize is rather by inference. The *Itala* palm, a unique variety especially identified with this area, is said to germinate only if the rock hard seeds, called "vegetable ivory", otherwise impossible to open, pass through the digestive system of an elephant. Since there are plenty of palms there must also be elephants, though we never saw them. Tracy says they walk across low water to these scattered islets and in general, maintain the relatively abundant presence of *Italas* along the riverbank. "You can see," Tracy adds, "that on the Zambia side there are no palms. They killed all their elephants." This is not true but it does illustrate the natural rivalry between the two neighboring countries. Tracy was of course unaware of the presence of "vegetable ivory", without the benefit of elephants, and the souvenir carvings in Costa Rica, among other ecological pilgrimage headquarters around the world.

That night after a barbecue dinner on the hotel terrace, scented with jasmine and mango, we followed the call of the *kudu* horn, which guided a parade of visitors to the dances, in a mock tribal village behind the Victoria Falls Hotel. A succession of numbers inspired in native Makishi and Shangaan ceremonies provoked loud "oohhhs" and "ahhhhs" of admiration, and I must say, the charm and humor and imaginative costumes—especially the crocodile, the lion and a really impressive "giraffe" on stilts— seemed harbingers of Julie Taymor's *Lion King.*

THURSDAY, NOVEMBER 9

Breakfast on the hotel terrace revealed a paucity of fresh fruit but an abundance of one of Britain's greatest contributions to civilization: tart citrus marmalade. There was a stunning variety to choose from, including kumquat, lime, lemon, grapefruit, Mandarin orange, Seville Orange, Valencia and blood orange, and if that was not enough, that towering, though non-citrus, delight: fresh ginger jam. The amazing discovery, on closer examination of the labels, revealed that all were packed in Zimbabwe. The other famous local product is Cream of Tartar, made from the ground bark of the *baobab* tree.

Tomás and I had decided to walk to Zambia. This is less dramatic than it sounds, since the border is only a kilometer and a half down the road. We started early, and even so, the heat was stifling, but my burns were better, in fact I had been allowed to sleep without bandages, so we were in a jovial frame of mind.

15.

BRIDGE INTO ZAMBIA

After checking out on the Zimbabwe side we had to cross the bridge, built in 1905, that amounts to a no-man's land, with the asphalt highway on one side and on the other, the railroad tracks.

Women shuffled along in groups of three or four, with shopping bags or suitcases on their heads. Men in shabby cheap suits carried parcels in woven plastic market bags. It was hard to tell if goods were coming or going, and it hardly mattered. Whatever was on one side the other wanted. And halfway across we were rewarded with a striking view of the gorge, with the Victoria Falls Hotel, like the image on those one-time steamer trunk labels, perched at the very end.

"You must declare even your gifts," says the customs official on the Zambian side, to the native woman with a sullen expression and a torn dress. She has a plastic shopping bag from which peeks a common metal teapot, table linen and groceries. Signs inside the wooden hut, papered on the walls, caution against unidentified packages or letters that might contain a bomb, marital infidelity as a health hazard and weapons traffic. We were now inside Zambia, formerly Northern Rhodesia.

We turn down a road to the Eastern Cataract, in order to photo-graph the falls from this side of the river, especially from the flimsy and heart-stopping metal footbridge over the chasm. Then we peek inside the small, unprepossessing museum, buy maps and guides, and continue our walk along the highway toward the Mosi-oa-Tunya Hotel. We are surprised to see a really charming, brightly spruced white building set in a carefully manicured garden, with swimming pool and welcome refreshments. The BBC film crew is staying here as well as the rafting teams, which the following day will tackle the great river, as it flows southward just beyond the flower beds.

We hire a taxi to drive us ten kilometers up the road to the nearest town, called, most appropriately, Livingstone. This corner of Zambia, very calm and rural, was dotted with flame trees: erup-tions of vermillion on the flat, red earth.

A riot of cicadas, breathy in the heat of the morning, drowns out the hum of the townspeople, in and around the tax-free stores, the railroad museum, the blanket factory, the Catholic church, the tex-tile mill, the storehouses for the maize, fruit and vegetable crops. The landmark North Western Hotel, one of the last vestiges of British colonial architecture seasoned with Art Decó, was built in 1900 just before completion of the rail line and during the height of the second Boer (or "Freedom") War of 1899–1902, just before the death, in January of 1901, of the much-loved Queen Victoria, after a reign of sixty-three years.

The Livingstone Museum is small, but careful and loving, with ethnographic displays referring to the indigenous tribes and their customs—a parallel of the dances we had seen the night before—along with a documentation of local flora and fauna, and, most interesting, a detailed breakdown of trade routes and development from the third century A.D., when Egypt pursued the Land of Punt, and was followed by the Romans, and possibly the Chinese, as well. Europeans entered the continent beginning with the Portuguese in the fifteenth century, the exploitation of ivory and copper, the Arab slave trade and later, the obsession with gold and diamonds, that continues to the present.

It is, nonetheless, with Livingstone that we are concerned. The Scottish missionary, anti-slave campaigner, cartographer, writer, in the best Victorian tradition of the encyclopedic mind, had remained a long time in Africa, assisted in his later, frail years by two native boys who foraged for food, carried him when he was too weak to walk, and stayed by him when the end was obviously near.

He was presumed to have died in the area of Ilala, near the village of chief Chitambo, in the swamps southeast of Lake Bangweulu in present-day Zambia, on May 1, 1873, of the effects of malnutrition, chronic malaria and internal bleeding caused by repeated bouts of dysentery, as well as hemorrhoids, but of course this is conjecture, based on Stanley's time with him and the corresponding notes in Stanley's journals. The version of the two boys, Chuma and Suza Mniasere, can nevertheless be verified. They knew the doctor was devoted to Africa and would want a part of himself to remain forever in his "Dark Continent", but they also knew he was a man of importance among his own kind. They cut out his heart and buried it under a Mvula or Mpundu tree, not far from where we are standing.

In their party was an African named Jacob Wainwright, a product of one of Livingstone's mission schools, who carved the inscription "LIVINGSTONE MAY 4 1873" and the names of the attendants, still visible on the tree. The Livingstone Memorial, built in 1899, marks the spot.

After removing the heart Chuma and Suza, accustomed to preserving hunted animals, also cleaned out his other vital organs, and embalmed the body in salts and herbs, wrapped it in grass matting and carried it on their shoulders, nearly twenty-five hundred kilometers to Zanzibar, where they delivered it to the British consul. Suza, baptized "David", remained for the rest of his life at the Christian mission in Zanzibar. Chuma returned to the burial site of

Livingstone's heart, sat himself down on the grave, and remained there, mourning until he died.

∫∫∫

Sylvester, our driver, took us back through the border and over the bridge, after staking us in local money to beer, soft drinks and museum admissions, which we settled in dollars along with his fee. He seemed more than gratified with the arrangement.

After clearing currency and customs on the Zimbabwe border we walked back up the road and through the woods to our hotel. We are accosted along the way by a veritable plague of vendors, hawking everything from dripping *Popsis*—fresh frozen natural fruit and most welcome in the heat—to wooden or soapstone hippos, rhinos, elephant, "malachite" beads that are really verdite, and clumsy necklaces of lopsided wooden animals. No matter how much or how sincerely we refuse to look at their merchandise the vendors make their appeal as if answering the telephone: "Yes? Good afternoon! Modern art? Giraffe tail? The elephant one? No? Have a nice day!"

We dash through the hotel sprinklers to cool off, steer free of the musing monkeys and have another soft drink by the pool. There seems no way to accumulate enough liquid to compensate for the eternal stream of perspiration that runs in rivulets down the spine.

∫∫∫

Tracy comes by to take us to the Crocodile Farm. Since there are only two of us she has brought two other passengers and hopes we have no objection. Both are vacationing nurses on contract to a maternity hospital, run by the army in Riyadh, Saudi Arabia. Janice is from Western Canada and Pauline, born in Surrey, is now called Asma since her conversion to Islam. I had seen her around the hotel grounds, in white tennis shoes and pale blue cotton pants, a white blouse and her black Muslim headscarf pinned tightly under her chin. It made her transparent turquoise eyes in the milky white face seem brighter and accentuated the anomaly in her decision. "I just thought I was missing something," she explained to me later. "I wanted a religion that gave me purpose, every day of my life, or perhaps made me feel needed." This is in direct contrast to the popular assumption, utterly false, that Islam is disdainful of women. "Women are not *less*, in the Muslim faith," says Asma, "they simply fill a different role. They do not exhibit themselves in public. They are instructed not to provoke men outside their household. They are a treasure, not to be spent foolishly. The Koran explains everything and leaves nothing to chance and yet it is constantly interpreted by people who presume to understand the Prophet's intentions, which were, incidentally, the protection of women, the guarantee of their legal rights, and their place of honor in the home. It is fanatics and madmen who have distorted all this to their own political purpose or their sexist ambitions, or plain, sadistic cruelty."

At the Crocodile Farm we were treated to a crash course in the care and feeding of future belts, purses, portfolios and briefcases, as ostensibly production of the animals is sufficient to guarantee survival, and the durability of the species. A shop on the premises offers the sale of crocodile products made right here, to reinforce the statement. There are certainly enough crocodiles in the wild, as we later witnessed along the Zambezi River and which we were to see again at Lake Kariba.

Crocodiles, amazing as it may seem, are related to birds. The Chinese claim to have found fossilized "dragons" covered with incipient feathers, as opposed to scales.

Crocodiles can live up to one hundred years, remain under water for over an hour if necessary and despite the myth, do not eat rotten meat. As a matter of fact, they are cannibals. The tiny ones, babies of six to nine months, are like smooth, rubbery toys.

16.

CAROL WITH BABY CROCODILE

A full grown male, however, is something to be reckoned with and can weigh as much as five hundred kilos. There is a great difference between the Nile crocodile here—the legendary Sobek of the ancient Egyptians—and its American cousin, the cayman or alligator. They are related but belong to divergent families. It would seem all the animals have their Asian, African and American counterparts. The only outsiders come from Australia, where nothing is related to anything else on earth.

The crocodile farm also serves as a modest refuge for orphaned cats. Whether or not any breeding in captivity is managed we have no idea, but the species are displayed in pairs: two servals, two leopards, two cheetahs, two wild cats. The latter look exactly like gray tabby housecats except that their claws are not retractable.

We were invited that evening to another display of native dances, at a cultural center down the road from the hotel, but my burns were bothering me and both legs were peeling. It had been a long day. We had tea in the English pub upstairs, skipped dinner and went to bed early.

FRIDAY, NOVEMBER 10

My birthday began not with Dylan Thomas' water birds but with a spray of bougainvillea blooms on my breakfast plate, a book on Zimbabwe Tomás had secretly bought in Harare, and a bronze mold of a scorpion on the paw print of an elephant, very heavy, that he had carried from the shop at the Mt. Kenya Safari Club. Now I would have to carry it in my suitcase and I carry it still. It sits on my desk opposite my computer.

After breakfast on the terrace Tracy took us over to the airfield for a "Flight of the Angels" on a Piper *Aztec,* fitting choice of aircraft, but just as we were about to board the flight was aborted due to a "technical malfunction". We repaired instead to the shopping streets of Vic Falls and unexpectedly found, in a shop otherwise devoted to comic t-shirts and canvas tote bags with painted giraffes, an intricate and remarkably dexterous wood carving of what looked like a scepter, with a snake standing on its tail, tightly coiled up to the neck, with an intent look in its beady little eyes and its tongue sticking out.

We asked Tracy about it and she explained it as "a rather stylized interpretation of *Nyami-Nyami* the River God, spirit of the Zambezi, who supposedly thwarts man's efforts at his domination and subverts the attempts to subjugate his people." This is what she said. Was she teasing us? Was this just an enterprising souvenir, an artistic cut above the clumsy woodcarvings on the bridge? Perhaps, after all, it was just a legend, to tempt the tourist.

I got another "happy birthday", this time sung in Africaans by a friend of Tracy's who went with us to the airport. It started to rain. There was that rich scent of the grateful red earth, and exploding greenery, as we departed for the game park in Hwange, after a slight delay, on the British Aerospace 146. With minor turbulence the flight took longer than it should: if not for the bad roads we might have driven, but the flight was already booked. Changes are unwise, especially in Africa.

We are now just twenty minutes from the fifteen thousand square kilometer conservation area in the sandy northeastern corner of the grand Kalahari Desert. Hwange National Park is home of the South African kudu antelope, sable antelope, blue wildebeest, banded mongoose, the southern giraffe, local impala and the Chacma baboon, among other regional species. We are taken off the airplane and right onto a game drive, before we can catch our breath.

For the log: two red-crested *koharen;* more *duiker* than we have seen before; red-billed *francolin;* several ostrich, crowned crane, guinea fowl and Egyptian geese. An approachable wart hog that posed for a photo. A female water buck. A family of three square-lipped white rhino in the deepening shadows of late afternoon: a mother, her baby, and a rejected adolescent son following dolefully behind the other two. In silhouette against the lavish African sunset of my birthday sky, the rare sable antelope, a local species here referred to as just "sable". The highly territorial males meet the females only for mating. And in the gathering dark, a shadowy herd of Cape buffalo.

As the sunset fades and the waxing moon appears to bathe the entire landscape with its coppery light, the car going into the camp ahead of us breaks an accelerator band. We stop to help. The night is ghostly and silent except for insects and a bat overhead. When the other car's damage is finally repaired we are able to go on, deeper into the brush on a narrow, sandy track, until we reach a clearing and a young bull elephant, ears flapping, blocks our way. We drive straight toward him and Raphael, our driver, turns the headlights full on his swaying bulk. He parries and moves off. It seems obvious that Raphael knows the animal, and his familiarity is contagious.

We drive on under the canopy of moon and stars until suddenly we come upon a large pool where four elephants are bathing and wallowing, reveling in the water. The young bull reappears, behind us now, trumpets, then walks around the car to defend his baby, while the family continues to frolic in the moonlight. We are breathless.

We arrive at camp, jubilant, but very late, and narrowly avoid the swimming pool, which is completely fenced. A sign explains: "For child safety, no gate. Climb over, please". The Sikumi Tree Lodge lies on a knoll overlooking a grassy plain. Three main structures are built in a row in the local native style, almost like Quonset huts with the roof rounded down until it also forms the walls. A curved line to one side is cut away to permit admittance. The first of these buildings is the lounge, the second the dining room and the third the office and shop. The rest of the compound consists in similar structures, but reached by climbing wooden stairs that lead straight up into the trees, to a two-room tree house—bedroom and bath. Facilities are rustic and rudimentary but hardly primitive. There is an electric blanket, mosquito netting but very little light, even in the daytime. A single electric bulb hangs from the ceiling, adorned with a woven basket shade that further reduces its effectiveness. The light is intended as well for the bathroom, in turn shielded from the bedroom not by a wall but by a perforated partition, a kind of Masonite scrim. There is another light bulb over the sink but it does little for the inside of the modular plastic stall shower. The rough floor boards are unfinished, and a good view of the sand and grass below is provided between the slats. The rooms, in effect, are for sleeping, nothing more, and I was selected for the bed placed right up against the slanted trunk of the tree that held us in the air. Tomás was afraid he would bump his head in the night.

After dumping our bags and going through the motions of settling in, we scrambled back down the ladder, minced across the dark lawn and found other people in the lounge. We are sweaty, rumpled and tired. Still, there is some of my birthday left. Our host, and owner of the lodge, Alan Elliot, was serving drinks. "Good evening," I called. "It's my birthday and we saw *five* elephants playing in a pool."

Everyone started to laugh at me, pointing fingers and guffawing. I thought them officious and impolite, until Alan Elliot, "The Elephant Man of Hwange", explained. It seems he had taken out a group in his truck and they had chanced on a major part of the herd at the same water hole, about fifty-two head of the eighty-five in the area, from among the well over two hundred in Hwange. Alan knew most of them personally. "I raised them," he said. "And they remember."

Fifty-two! No one had spoken a word, they said, no one had breathed. Anyone wearing white had to duck down. The Land Rover eased into the edge of the pool, with water covering the wheels, then they idled the engine in reverse gear, just in case, and stayed there observing fifty-two bulls, cows and calves at their evening ablutions. Fifty-two! The indifferent elephants brushed against the Land Rover, inspected the passengers with a tentative poke of the trunk, sniffled and huffed, then went on with their bath, and all the time the half dozen people with Alan never whispered, never blinked, never shifted their feet or scratched a mosquito bite; they were paralyzed and breathless in wonder and awe, and my envy.

I think I was so madly jealous I could hardly talk, until a woman in a t-shirt and windbreaker, stooping over the bar, raised her head. "Hi! I'm Josephine, Alan's wife. Happy birthday. Tell us about your five elephants." They had been the last of the bathers. The rest had earlier lumbered off into the underbrush.

There was nothing left but to have dinner. Everyone serves his own plate from a buffet around the campfire, then takes it into the dining hut to sit at one of four long tables—two down one side, two down the other—and that was the end of it, until the chattering kitchen staff appeared with a birthday "cake", a corner cut out of the community dessert, decorated with flowers from the garden and a stubby candle, the kind used by the guests when the electricity was lost in a power outage. Everyone sang "Happy Birthday" until Tomás remembered the Swahili: *Si kukuni yako.* Or, if you prefer, *Sikuku ni yako.* No one seems to agree on the pronunciation.

SATURDAY, NOVEMBER 11

I thought I heard a lion nearby grunting through the night and well into the dawn but we have seen no lions, nor in fact any felines. One of the guests in a neighboring hut was up and dressed and doing Tai-Chi when we climbed down the ladder for morning tea at the campfire. Josephine calls out, "Be careful of the handle on the kettle in the coals".

Breakfast was served as dinner had been: a buffet by the fire pit. Afterward we moved director's chairs onto the slope of the knoll, for a better view of the plain. Impala leaping and frolicking are followed by two wart hogs and a line of six sables. Temerous, they descend to the water hole, sniffing the wind. A brush fire sweeps across the line behind the trees, that passes for a horizon. Is this a firebreak or is all of Africa in flames?

Raphael appears with the car and we head out for a game drive. We pass a herd of female sables at their grazing. The calves are hidden nearby, Raphael explains. More sable cross the path farther along, then zebra, more impala and wart hog. This is a fanciful world, Alice Through the Looking Glass, populated by improbable beings going about their natural business. Everywhere there are kudu and ground hornbills, steenbuck, yellow-billed kites, bullfrogs and a large tortoise. A solitary bull elephant at a green pool, covered with mud from a luscious bath, disdainfully urinates while he calculates the distance between us. Then he gingerly samples the thorny food, tosses his ears and head, waves his trunk at us, and finally, having left a message for whoever follows, turns his back to shuffle away.

Another herd of sable at ten o'clock, the bounding youngsters like dressage horses, prancing and smart. In the three largest breeds of antelope—eland, roan and sable—both males and females have horns. From the kudu down only the males have horns. A bachelor group of adolescent impalas crosses the field, leaping and bounding among the termite mounds, which are gigantic, integrated into the roots of the smaller trees. As the heat rises the animals move into the shade of the wooded copses. We come upon a kudu herd—one dominant male and his females—under a tree, the fruit bats hanging soft and tawny, completely asleep, upside-down in the branches over their heads.

Four young bull elephants, about fifteen to twenty years old, their male organs hanging down while they laze in the shade, are scratching their wrinkled rumps against the tree branches and stumps. They rumble and snort at us while we observe them, so close the dust of their puffing and blowing covers our faces, filling our nostrils with their musky scent. Their legs are crossed and they lurch drunkenly, the tender caress of one long trunk on another's back, ears flapping gently, the spine making a keel-like ridge along their hips. They lean into each other, never still, rubbing and scratching all the time. We are only ten meters away. The game in the park enjoys relative freedom and safety but in return must tolerate this persistent persecution by the tourist vehicles, the staring eyes, the cameras and binoculars, the invasion of its privacy. Do they care? Perhaps they enjoy the company of this insolent, upright ape, or take pleasure in the riddle: Who turns toward? Who turns away? Who stands his ground defensively?

We had been too long without a puncture. Raphael gets down to change the tire while the dragonflies and hornets close in. The heat rises as from a wide-open oven door. A wart hog goes wallowing, to cool off in the pond just to one side of where we stand to watch. A cloud of little white butterflies lifts on the breeze like a school of fish, turns as one, flirts, departs.

The tire is changed now. We stop for a soft drink at an observation platform over a waterhole, facing the teak forests that provide the center poles for Sikumi's huts. On the burnt-out plain, scourged by the fire, the "secretary bird", or "serpent eagle", completely in his element, scuffs across the surface in pursuit of snakes. A hawk-eagle overhead swoops down on his prey, a rat fleeing the still burning stubble. Why are there no felines?

We return to the hotel for lunch, to discover the news of the opening of the Berlin Wall. Everyone is chattering, commenting as if with great authority, prophesying the future of Germany. The news has reached us at the ends of the earth, where letters once took months, even years, if at all, to arrive at their destination, and meantime the world went on spinning, things changed or not and something world-shaking elsewhere had no bearing here.

Asma and Janice have caught up with us. They fall into the boarding house friendliness, while Alan Elliot amuses us with stories of the animals he has filmed, classified and protected. Everyone begins on South African politics, theories regarding Great Zimbabwe, the economic success story of Botswana, the sweet and loving nature of the Bushmen, the textile industry in the country's second city of Bulawayo which at that time manufactured safari wear for Banana Republic. Idle chat, campfire chat.

SUNDAY, NOVEMBER 12

It was the middle of springtime in the Southern Hemisphere, and it had rained all night. Toadstools appeared, as if by magic, in the grass and across the sandy expanse under the tree house.

We drove out in the drizzle through a neighbor's farm, among his grazing cattle. He was a white Africaans farmer, a carryover from the Rhodesia days, but later, by letter, we learned his holdings has been expropriated and he, with his family, had been expelled from the country. Raphael, our normally resourceful guide, had put up the canvas top on the Land Rover but it leaked. Tomás opened his umbrella inside the car and we all laughed.

A game drive was unlikely in this weather so Raphael suggested taking us into the villages of the *Matabele* (*Ma* means "many") or "*Ndebele*", to see first hand how the people in the area live. His people. We find it hard to believe that this tall, articulate, attractive and self-assured black boy, with the clear gaze and the careful knowledge of so much of the area's lore, was born in a round hut in the bush. *Why* is it hard to believe? If we presume to be so devoted to self-determination, is it only possible in the West, and maybe since Mandela in South Africa, to surmount obstacles, deal with the challenges of everyday existence, and overcome superstition and prejudice?

Despite the dictators, life in Africa was simpler in 1989. There was hope and optimism throughout the continent. There was, as yet, a nominal faith in Robert Mugabe's government. He was the first democratically elected authority in Zimbabwe after Independence. He was one of the few democratically elected government leaders to *survive* Independence, anywhere in Sub-Saharan Africa. How were we to know that a quarter of a century later he would still be in power? And AIDS, now a scourge, was initially only an occasional rumor. It was still happening to someone else, in the *next* village. The people here, in *this* village, were able to begin *their* day, as they always had, with a typical meal: *sadza,* a corn porridge served with a "relish", that is, assorted vegetables. They washed the whole thing down with tea, if they could afford it, and if not, with plain water, often boiled over the cooking fire. The hearty midday dinner, which is the main meal eaten in the late afternoon when the family is reassembled after the day's activities, could also consist of *sadza,* this time with meat, if available, and perhaps more vegetables.

The villagers customarily lived by bartering goods or services at the General Store in the township, and thus obtained pots, flour, sugar, cloth, salt, or whatever else they needed. Fields were farmed more for personal consumption and small-time barter than for the broad scale marketing of the produce. Women carried twenty-five liter containers on their heads, no small task, to collect water from a hand pump, or to channel off water for cattle or for washing clothes at a trough: a social hour, the one really compatible time of day for them. Their routine was laborious but relatively simple. They worked the fields in the early morning, then went for water and gossip, and afterward returned home to "fill pots" (prepare the meal), before going out again to the fields. They also cultivated small patches of vegetables for their "relish", except during periods of drought, when these had to be sacrificed and the roots, bark or stems used for firewood.

We saw nothing around us to suggest a religious observance. Possibly the missionaries, both Christian and Muslim, had missed this corner of Zimbabwe, this sandy patch of the Kalahari. Ancestral traditions included the worship of a demon figure, but if appeased by offerings of cloth and beads, tossed to his "reflection" in the nearby river, he showed the dead, buried with ceremonies invoking his name, the road to heaven, which is otherwise impassable. This "demon" is most likely a regional version of Nyami-Nyami, the River God, whom we would encounter again, later in our travels, in which case the road to heaven unfolded along the dancing waters of a coursing stream.

Provided the deceased had behaved well during a lifetime on earth and among the villagers, he was entitled to a future life. Here, as elsewhere in the world, the key problem twenty-some years ago was alcohol, and while today alcoholism is rampant and drugs are also an issue, there is no question that alcohol and tobacco have killed more people and destroyed more lives than any other addictive narcotic, a fact well noted by the Prophet Muhammad, whose doctrine, as Asma reminds us, demands temperance.

On the ground: giant ants. In the bush: the braying of donkeys and the clanging of goats' bells as the background for the Sunday morning bustle in the clusters of round grass huts or mud-brick dwellings with thatched roofs, that make up the communities or villages. Children up to the age of twelve sleep with their grandmother, who raises them. At puberty, the boys are separated from the girls. The new generation of girls had learned a little English but the parents and grandparents spoke only their local dialect.

Women and children were dressed in worn but modern Western-style clothing, often complemented by knitted wool or acrylic yarn caps. We were allowed to photograph the baby. She was called *Tandikille* which, we were told, meant "Loveliness".

The sleeping huts had metal doors. Since safety hardly seemed a factor in a grass hut I had to assume this kept out the scratching chickens or gave the door greater durability. Raphael was unable to explain. He said he had never thought about it.

$$\int\int\int$$

The mother sleeps with the father during her childbearing years. A man is still allowed many wives and, with each wife, the children she produces. No one has ever taught them the dangers of overpopulation. They still believed there would always be enough food, and if they had many children, their village would be more important than all the others. The village in which we find ourselves amounted to a single, extended, family. There are six youngsters and four women: the man's sister, her mother (not the same, we are told, as *his* mother) and two wives. One of the wives is pregnant. She does a little dance for us. She is flirtatious and graceful. Her movements are, in fact, astonishing, exactly like those in any contemporary discotheque, in complete control and with unerring natural rhythm.

There is a great deal of coughing and shoving of goats in the cooking area, kept isolated from the sleeping area, off to one side of the cluster of huts. A separate structure, the granary, is divided into four compartments, also kept apart from the sleeping areas.

One compartment is for maize, another for millet, a third for sorghum and the last for anything around that needs to be stored.

We are given a demonstration of millet grinding in a clearing under the shade trees, using a long wooden pestle in a tub made from a hollowed tree stump. The process takes at least twenty minutes, nonstop, of rhythmic and unrelenting pounding, while the scrawny chickens and a bony puppy go wild, scrambling for the crumbs that fly from the mortar. The sudden appearance of a hawk-eagle sends them for cover but as soon as the predator passes they are back, clucking and snatching at bits of millet, while they keep a wary eye out for the bird's return.

During those years a primary school for the two hundred and ninety-one youngsters in the township area was offered on either a day or a boarding basis, at no charge for children from one to seven years of age. Teachers were recruited from among the various villages and might live on the school premises. Books were scarce, the quality of the printing poor, and they were expensive, as in most of the undeveloped world, but especially here, as we had discovered in Harare, in Arusha, in Nairobi, in Livingstone, just about anywhere we had been in Africa. This is a problem that grew more acute after liberation from the universally rapacious and mostly unapologetic European colonizers. In 1989 it was different. Children still had their arms and legs. They went to classes. Lessons were usually memorized or posted on a blackboard and reinforced with written exercises, exactly as I had seen in Southeast Asia or Latin America: as in Laos or Cambodia, in Peru, in Honduras, in Guatemala.

The best of the children's written exercises were displayed on the schoolroom wall, along with any practical items, such as household articles, that might have been assembled. The education department contributed whatever teaching aids it could muster. Alphabet cards, for example, described "z" for Zulu, and "m" for "merry monkey". Sayings for the older children: "A good man's mind is like a good hotel, always open". Many lessons were taught through music and song, a popular expression, but vocabulary was learned by rote like anywhere else. The "f": *faka, fika, fihla, fohla, fethu, futha, fikela, fafaza.*

The school term lasted three months. Since a man might have twenty-five children in school at any given time, perhaps three in each term, the wives all helped, especially if someone was ill, but both the family and the State were hard pressed to find the funds to continue an education past the age of seven, especially in a dictatorship, where funds are needed elsewhere.

The buildings were humble and crumbling. Roofs, of laminated metal assembled in orderly, oversized shingles, protected the little houses, which on this day, being Sunday, a day of rest for the children, housed the goats. An "orchard garden" was in progress, as well as a school project in the form of a scale model, created by the children in bricks and pebbles, that referred to Great Zimbabwe, one of the most controversial and, to this day unfathomable, archaeological sites of the world.

Just beyond the schoolyard lies the soccer field. This is an important facet of attending school, especially as far as the older boys are concerned. The school stands adjacent to other facilities, and though privately owned, might be considered the domain of the community. There is the tick trough for cattle and a mill of concrete and brick that the owner is happy to rent for the grinding of flour. A public health poster tacked to the outside wall showed a concerned mother with her child, asking the nurse if the impending vaccination was for TB, polio, measles or whooping cough. "Always explain", admonishes the poster. A sign on the little brick monument as we depart the school grounds, crudely painted in white letters against a blue background, proclaims: "A pilgrim's reward is the memory of having been there."

No need to bid long goodbyes to Asma and Janice; they will catch up with us at Fothergill Island. Alan and Raphael drop us the at the airstrip, for the short flight to Kariba, at that time the second-largest (after Aswan, in Egypt) man-made lake in the world. And, following Egypt's reasoning, Zimbabwe's engineers also projected electricity and progress. They got more of the former than the latter. They created a vast and desolate world of creeping fingers of water, that crawled into the niches and crevices of the central plateau that were swelled by the Zambezi's normal annual overflowing. But then, according to serious believers, it was Nyami-Nyami, the River God, who rebelled. A succession of flood seasons, each more severe than the last, time and again washed out the construction. Then the years of drought lowered the lake's level, revealing thousands of dead trees, pointing the accusing fingers of their parched branches at the blighted landscape.

What remains, instead of a thriving recreational area, residential subdivisions, hotels and golf club, is a paradise for crocodiles, tens of thousands of which populate the shore, according to the warning signs directed at would-be swimmers.

The official story from both Zambia and Zimbabwe, who share the lake as they do the river and the massive Victoria Falls it creates, still supports the wisdom in the decision to develop the dam, and offers statistics verifying the benefits to industry and agriculture, despite evidence to the contrary.

We stayed in one of the "luxury" hotels actually inaugurated by Queen Mother Elizabeth, such was the enthusiasm invested in the project. The Caribbea Bay Hotel and Casino certainly consumed enough electricity to justify the dam, having selected for a design, instead of materials and construction consistent with the steamy climate and rocky terrain, an unfortunate architecture more congruent in North Africa or New Mexico, properly indicated for the desert, and only kept reasonably tolerable by the outlay of outrageous quantities of air conditioning.

More electricity ran the slot machines, which were devoid of customers. The place was grimy and had gone shabby, despite the pretensions of a layout for a family holiday. Its most peculiar feature, furthermore, was the Mexican restaurant, "Pedro's", where the waiters were dressed as Texas cowboys, convinced that this is what people in Mexico looked like.

It was thought that gambling and water sports would bring in great quantities of foreign exchange but the results had been disappointing. An ambitious wooden pier was additionally confected for pleasure craft, but the diminishing level of the lake left it too far above the water line to serve any practical purpose. It looked instead like a forlorn abstract sculpture tacked onto the artificial shore.

MONDAY, NOVEMBER 13

The next day we decide to have a look at the dam, which created a lake supposedly two hundred and eighty kilometers long and an average of thirty-two kilometers wide. We hire a taxi for the morning, not easy to come by, but someone blissfully obliged us by descending from a car just as we were debating the idea of hiring it, having already been told by the management that no taxis were available.

We drove through nearby Andora Bay, a semi-abandoned would-be residential development where the Italian engineers lived during the construction of Kariba Dam, from 1960 to 1965. Zambia and Zimbabwe each generated their own electricity. New turbines, we were told, had been added to step up capacity. Both countries shared in the dam's maintenance. As always happens in dam building, a number of people had fallen into the concrete, amounting in this case to eighty-six, of various nationalities.

Other statistics, according to the plaque on the wall of the dam:

Height: 420 feet
Length of crest: 2050 feet
Thickness: 80 feet
Volume of concrete: 1375 million cubic yards
Spillway discharge: 336,000 cubic feet or 2.1 million gallons/second
Storage capacity: 150 acre feet (41 million millions)
Six turbines of 140,000 BHP
18,000 volt generators 3/240,000 KVA
890 miles of 330,000 volt transmission lines feeding six major substations.

♫♫

We stopped at a lookout and information office above the dam wall to visit a shop, to examine the local crafts. Tomás was hoping to find another portrait in wood of Nyami-Nyami, the River God, surely the "demon" figure worshipped by the Matabele. "A carving is a carving," he likes to say, and the art of working stone or wood is always worthy of note. And he has un erring eye. He manages to single out the piece of note, whatever really warrants attention.

17.

CARVED STAFFS: NYAMI-NYAMI THE RIVER GOD

He found an enormous staff, authentic or otherwise, and taller than a man, carved from top to bottom, quite delicately and very elaborately, fashioned of a single branch of a tree. It supposedly told the entire story of the River God, his people, their hunger and thirst, their tribulations as a result of the construction of the dam and the debacle as far as their farmlands were concerned.

After hearing the legend in great detail we could understand Nyami-Nyami's rage, and would learn more of it as time went on. Nyami-Nyami is normally portrayed with the head of a fish and the body of a serpent, whose coils are presumably the waves of the water. He represents sustenance and was opposed from the outset, say the locals, to the building of the dam. In fact, he did everything in his power to confound engineers and government officials. All attempts to distract him, however, were destined to fail, given the endless bureaucracy, as well as the timetable among all the countries—Zambia, Zimbabwe, Mozambique, Malawi—affected by the project. In actual fact, says our taxi driver, no one knows all that much about Nyami-Nyami, what he likes or dislikes, and no one knows how big he really is, the taxi driver tells us, "as he never completely shows himself."

Nyami-Nyami's emissary in spirit, according to the lady in the shop, is *Mudzimu*, a deity of the Tonga elders; he is entrusted with the specific task of appeasing the River God and his consort, who until disturbed by the dam project lived blissfully in the Kariwa Gorge. When the two gods were finally coerced into allowing the Great Dam Wall to be built, it was *Mudzimu's* further responsibility to comfort the divine couple, elaborate on the deficiencies of the project yet convince them that despite its shortcomings, in the end the dam would be beneficial, and everything would turn out right. Nonetheless, Nyami-Nyami was furious, and remains so. Everyone attests to this, but not everyone remembers about it all the time.

∫∫∫

The taxi, in which we had stashed our bags, finally drops us at the boat landing for Fothergill Island. We thought we had been booked to fly over but it seems air service was abandoned three years earlier. While we waited for the boat to arrive I decide to look around, though there is precious little to see, despite the enormity of the area adjacent to the lake or the ambitions to have been realized there. Most of the steep hills, rocky and bare, drop right down to the water's edge. The few beaches were artificially confected from a truckload or two of gravel. Vegetation is sparse. Construction is sporadic, maybe a few houses –most of them abandoned—and here and there a hotel or two, also empty.

These enterprises would appear to have been initiated with a great spurt of time and money before both petered out. To reach the boat landing we had to turn off the main highway and then lurch along a dirt track, very hot and dusty. There is only a small wooden dock on pontoons, and a short distance away a thatched shelter, which serves as a waiting room. It has no chairs or benches but two logs have been dragged into the shade and left there, for anyone who wants to sit on them.

In time the speedboat arrived. Despite the cautionary sign at the Caribbea Bay Hotel no one is wearing a life jacket. The bumpy ride, twenty-six kilometers across the lake, which normally takes half an hour, took nearly fifty minutes since the water, as the boat-man tried to explain, was more choppy than usual. We thought nothing of it, but the other passengers included a tiny woman from South Africa, who was terrified, and who spent the entire crossing clinging to Tomás as if her life depended on it. And maybe it did. Our other companions included her more robust sister and a tall, good-humored Australian, from Perth. John was a widower on holiday.

Except at mealtimes we never saw the sisters again but we got to know John quite well before our adventure was over. Very shaken and battered by the slapping of the flat-bottomed boat on the rough, wind-tossed water, we at last pulled into a quiet cove and tied up at a rickety little dock. A large sign with a paw-print on it, by way of a logo, announced that this was Fothergill. It was later explained that this *had* been an island and is still called that, but the receding water left part of the original land exposed. It can be reached now by road but it is a long way around, as we were soon to learn.

A large truck, with no top or sides, furnished with rows of metal benches instead of seats, was waiting to collect all of us, along with our baggage, to take us to the Lodge. A look around revealed a mournful landscape, with dead trees leering at us from the water's edge, making navigation not only difficult but very dangerous. A herd of Cape buffalo on a bucolic field, despite their reputation as Africa's most dangerous animal, grazed indifferently behind a cluster of huts in the foreground. Beyond the boat landing, on a spongy knoll, three young native girls, each with a plastic bucket, were collecting frogs. Our driver, a surly red-neck in green fatigues, high socks and desert boots—seemingly standard garb for the "island"—introduced himself as "Richard".

Having assembled everyone he put the truck in gear, drove one hundred and fifty meters up a dirt track over a knoll, then stopped in front of the cluster of huts we had seen from the landing. "Here we are," he said cheerily, climbing ceremoniously down from the driver's seat. A boy then scrambled onto the truck and began tossing out the baggage to another boy, who left everything neatly stacked in orderly rows next to the front wheels, where each passenger could collect his own belongings. It seemed an unusual procedure. Today this would have been attributed, perhaps, to a question of security, but back then I think it was just a shortage of personnel. Or plain indifference.

We found ourselves near the office, in front of a pole-and-thatch pavilion with an empty swimming pool and deserted deck, affectionately referred to by the knowing as "The Termite Mound". Below it, on a lower level, were the camp-style dining room and a doleful gift shop, empty and long-ago abandoned. Up a flight of wooden stairs, on the lookout level, was the bar, where the "sundowner" was a tradition.

In addition to a collection of miniature flags from the countries of the Lodge's various patrons, decoration consisted only of the local "tiger fish" from nearby Sanyati Gorge, stuffed and mounted, formidable animals with fearsome teeth, though only about seventy or eighty centimeters long. Probably distant cousins to the *pirañas* of the Amazon.

The spaces between the huts, all around the hotel compound, were occupied by genuine termite mounds. These towered two to three meters into the air, up the trunks and into the branches of the tender young trees that served as shade for the bungalows.

18.

TERMITE MOUNDS ON FOTHERGILL ISLAND

We had been alerted by Abercrombie and Kent to the fact that our accommodations consisted of "tasteful and charming native-style huts" with "adjacent showers", so we had visions of tiptoeing across the grass in rubber sandals, clutching our robes around our bodies, the way lit by fireflies, but the problem here, instead of architectural, was only a matter of semantics. Both toilet and shower were attached to the rooms and were completely private, with access from the bedroom. Strictly speaking they occupied extensions of the main sleeping area but were open to the starry night and unburdened by a roof. In effect, they were simply open-air bathrooms. The toilet, in fact, was reached through a stable-style door, which opened *into* the bedroom and therefore collided with the beds, making it necessary to climb *over* the bed to get into the cubicle. Either that, or hurdle the lower half of the stable door.

The grass roof, like a helmet, curved to form the walls. Halfway down it ran into a stone barrier, built at right angles to the concrete foundation. Part of the grass thatch had been nibbled away by the neighborly buffalo that grazed at will. There are no doors so if anyone, including a buffalo, wants to come in he says "Knock-Knock". So much for ecological tourism.

The dressing table, on the other hand, afforded a swivel mirror. Definitely, creature comforts. The closet, meanwhile, consisted of a pole with two wire hangers, already crooked and deformed. A Bible in the dressing table drawer had water damage. It was ragged and full of dead insects, like everything else, after just a few moments with the light on. This condition extended to hat, jacket, shoes and mosquito net, which had more flies and mosquitoes inside than out. The netting, however, was dark green. We discovered, to our delight, that the suffocating sensation of the other netting in our African experience, just as it had been in Belize or Brazil, was due to the white color, which at night is overly visible. The dark green netting, after dark, even with the open sides of the hut and the moonlight that flooded into the room, was nearly invisible, therefore never claustrophobic.

Each hut had its own little terrace, facing the lake. This particular afternoon, however, was windy, nearly gale proportions. The waves on the shore rose up onto the grassland where the buffalo, unperturbed, continued to graze. It was a bleak and foreboding landscape, a russet moor dotted with green trees, and these tossed like sails on a stormy sea. Nyami-Nyami continued to rage.

Early the next morning we were called by two ladies who run the place, Meg and Cora, in close-cropped hair and the standard khaki shorts, to a briefing in "The Termite Mound". Fothergill's principal attraction, they explain, is the walking safari or "walkabout", in this case accompanied by a trained naturalist, through the Matusadona Woodland, though this morning it could also be a combination walking and canoeing trip. We were informed, however, with a mixture of sadness and joy, that the licensed guide was away in Kariba, at the regional hospital, where his wife was having a baby. Everything would be done, nonetheless, to make our stay as pleasant and as informative as possible. "In fact," said Meg, rather sternly, "the whole interest of Fothergill is the involving of our guests in the local lore. No package holiday for our people. We were born here and we love this country. We want to share as much of it as we can."

Tomás and I were assigned to David, a very intent, nice-looking blond Zimbabwean boy, who aspired to his license as a full-fledged guide. He had trained for a long time and wanted to be able to take people around on "foot-safari". I wonder where all of them are now. Did Mugabe force them to leave the country? Did they remain? Are they prospering? Or, like so many others, have they lost everything?

𝕊𝕊𝕊

The "island", as a reserve, was created in 1958 by "Operation Noah", when the conservation area was officially constituted under Rupert Fothergill, director of the operation. Animals from all over the Kariwa Gorge were brought here, on the theory that since most species dislike water they would remain and adapt once the dam was flooded. Snakes, tortoise, birds, elephant, rhino, hippo, buffalo, impala, duiker, all the antelopes and in fact anything alive, were ferried to this spot in a massive attempt to reconcile conservation with the Kariba reclamation project.

Fothergill Island became a likely candidate for the experiment, at least in theory, because of its principal phenomena, the almost limitless incidence of *mopane* or "butterfly" plant, a versatile source of nourishment named for the unique shape of its leaf. This resinous scrub, high in protein, reacts with the alkaline content of the dense, red clay soil and provides food, though very little shade, for many of the species trying to survive here. Its slender branches can even be woven into a rope – a Bushmens' trick—but the elephants seem to dislike it, especially "Rory". According to David, "he is a real rascal, definitely a bit of a bad guy", so he tears up large quantities of *mopane* and leaves the devastated growth "just lying about, so it's no good to anyone. He won't eat it."

Since the lake began receding, not only from drought but from electricity spill-off, the "torpedo grass" along the edge has been exposed. "It makes good fodder," David explains, "and was able to live under water as long as it received sunlight so revived so very easily. The elephant seem to like it and it has become the mainstay of the buffalo that graze near the shore, as long as they don't get their ears wet. Conservation, you know, and resource management, are a tricky business."

Plants on the island play an important role in the total structure of survival, becoming as the case may be shelter, sustenance, liquid, even defense. The "cork bush", for example, which grows in the water, has an acid bark, that kills the fish when they try to eat it. Man, however, can neutralize the poisonous protein by simply boiling the dead fish, thus rendering it perfectly edible.

By contrast, the "southern milkweed butterfly", by virtue of its diet, becomes noxious to its enemies. The sour plum, on the other hand, is perfectly edible by any of the species, including man. It is juicy and refreshing, though offers little meat. In compensation the large seed, with its pungent almond flavor, is also edible; and the roots can be brewed as a cure for certain types of blood parasites originating in bad drinking water. The "monkey orange", another useful plant, grows to the size of a grapefruit and rattles when shaken. Only the pulp, however, is edible. The seeds contain strychnine.

A number of bird species enjoy the island and grace it with their lavish plumage, their exotic habits or the unlikely shrill of their astonishing call: the spur-wing geese, the sacred ibis, the glossy ibis, the black-winged stilt, the yellow-billed stork and the great white egret. The white-winged tern lives from picking insects off the surface of the ponds but turns "black-winged" during the breeding season. The lilac-breasted roller, one of Zimbabwe's favorites, is so called because of the male's acrobatic breeding antics. The Caspian plover and the carmine bee-eater nest in holes in the river banks. The red-winged *pratincole* shows a red flash when it flies and a black band, like a weeping eye, to protect its ground-nesting habits: it looks like a snake when its head is lifted.

The most remarkable of the ground nesters, however, is the Kitlitz'splover. This tiny, otherwise unprepossessing, bird pretends her wing is broken and that she cannot fly, in order to lure predators away from her nest. There is always the danger that her eggs will roast from the heat of the sun, so she kicks dirt over them with unimaginable speed, then limps and flutters a considerable distance away. When the curious intruder follows her she "recovers" in a flash and takes to the air. When the threat is past she goes back to the nest, with great dexterity scrapes the dirt off the eggs, and resumes her nesting. Unfortunately, in this case and on this day her brilliant ploy is partially futile: she has dug her nest exactly on the ridge between the two furrows that serve as a road and is therefore interrupted constantly, each time a car goes by.

The fish eagle is completely identified with the "island". The male is smaller than the female and his shriek, like a poignant seagull, is more shrill. Together they build their nest even in the broken bare trees of Fothergill and are much more affected by the commercial fishing on the lake than the other species. "They have become klepto-parasites," explains David. "They steal from the other birds." Yet unbeknownst to David, to this day I hear their scream in my dreams, and I yearn for Africa.

The beautiful Egyptian geese, with the smart white epaulets and their romantic nature—they fall in love and mate for life—are thinking of moving into a nest abandoned by a pair of fish eagles not currently breeding. "There was no posting of a re-zoning notice, however," explains David, "so they got chased out."

The stunning black egret spreads its wings like an umbrella to see into the water to look for fish; its yellow feet move in the pond to attract prey. The African *jacana*, on the other hand, uses its long toes to enable it to walk on the aquatic vegetation, earning it the name of "lily trotter". It nests and breeds in the weeds. One female requires the services of several males, which take turns incubating and caring for the eggs. If danger approaches the custodian of the moment will pick up the chicks and run with them for protection.

The territorial animals, like the impala, must use their wits as well as their scent glands, to compete for the best females. A dominant male, in order to assure the survival of his genes in the next generation, has to vanquish every challenger, or end his life in the ignominious "bachelor's club". The impala of Fothergill are nonetheless numerous, being both "browsers" and "grazers". The size and make-up of the herd depend on food and water supplies. Just as for humans these are known as "stress levels".

The shy duiker, by contrast, is the most widely distributed of the antelopes. It browses in the thick brush at night, eating very little because of its small size, and therefore requires no great volume of grass or brush. It can even derive a good share of its water supply from its food and is thus exceedingly adaptable. It also has a diverse appetite. If necessary it will even feed on worms or caterpillars.

We notice the waterbuck and ask David about their markings. Instead of the white ring on their rumps, as elsewhere, here their markings are a solid white, like a seat cushion. The oil in their heavy fur gives off a strong odor, much like sheep's lanoline: it is not only repugnant to their enemies but acts as waterproofing. It also helps them to float. Their babies, to their disadvantage, have no scent and have to be hidden in the brush, to protect them from predators.

A hippo lurches out of the water and moves toward us at about thirty-five kilometers an hour. We might have considered this to be threatening, but David assures us there is no danger. How can he be so sure? We are amazed at its agility, especially on land. Hippos here, like those farther north, produce a reddish "blood-sweat", says David, which acts as a suntan lotion, for "if they burn they become particularly bad-tempered". They normally feed at night, when the heat is down, eat the grass along the shore and are seriously territorial. They will fight, if necessary, to the death. They are traditionally, like their name, river animals, and since they dislike the rough water on the lake they remain, on these windy afternoons, close to the shore, especially on a day like this one, when a storm seems to be brewing.

The lake is well-known for its crocodiles, as the warning signs at the Caribbea Bay had indicated. The last census, taken four years earlier, registered thirty thousand in this area, two meters or larger in length, but one of these had been reported one hundred and twenty kilometers from the shore. Apparently he had roamed inland in search of food. If eggs are incubated at a lower temperature—twenty-six to thirty degrees centigrade—the hatchlings will be female. If temperatures reach thirty-one to thirty-four degrees centigrade the eggs will hatch male. The opposite occurs with the terrapin. The population division, says David, is thought to be related to the food supply or to other conditions necessary for survival.

We stop near the water's edge, along a grassy ridge, for a sundown beer in full view of the elephants, stubbing up the roots of the grass with their toes, unconcerned and indifferent. The elephant is born with six sets of molars. When one wears out another set moves into place. When none are left the animal is old and will starve, around sixty or seventy years of age. Elephants never stop growing so the largest in size is also the oldest in years. The circumference of the forefoot print is multiplied by seven and one half in order to presumably indicate the animal's height. The print made by the forefoot is round, by the rear oval. These almost overlap when the animal strides along, but not quite, unless the elephant is running. Since he scuffs there is no way to determine the direction he took. Elephants stride with a parallel step, instead of alternate, that is, with the two feet on the right side, then the two on the left. The skin on the bottom of their feet is wrinkled and leaves a unique print, as would a man's finger, unless they have been walked over hot pavement, as happens in parts of India, in which case the skin is burned and distorted, and is very painful. The foot splays when it comes down, with a layer of cartilage to muffle the sound, accommodating itself to the terrain and assuring a firm grip, especially on grassy or leafy ground. Rocky ground, however, is torture to an elephant, and can even kill the animal if a stone hits a pressure point. This was among the problems that confronted Hannibal when he took his elephants across the Alps.

Elephants usually sleep standing up, or leaning against a termite mound. They occasionally lie down for half an hour or so, in order to rest, then rise again with great difficulty. The slit opening forward of the ears is intended for hearing. The enormous fans really consist of a web of veins that cools the air by several degrees, before it reaches the brain. More agitated flapping, however, is a danger signal, David reminds us, in effect a warning to intruders.

We return to the hotel under the vivid canopy of a surly sky, striated around the edges with the angry tones of bruised flesh. We shower under the stars and the light from the brazen moon, nearly full, its light filling the whole sky and reflecting off the lake. The persistent braying of the geese through the night, the geckos rustling in the grass thatch ceiling, and buffalo grazing in the doorway, were familiar now.

TUESDAY, NOVEMBER 14

Despite the clear night, which should have augured a good day, the next morning was moody and very windy, the lake even more choppy than before. Insects in the shifting light of dawn and small animals in the thatch came to life with a symphony of scratching and pawing. Since the sink is outside with the shower there are ants in my toothbrush.

Anyone who has read about Africa, or seen movies, from *Mogambo, Tarzan* and *Greystoke to King Solomon's Mines, The Snows of Kilimanjaro, The Ghost and* the *Darkness, The Green Hills of Africa, Mountains of the Moon* and *Out of Africa,* has heard the term "spoor" and has wondered what it means. Is it the animal's hoof print, like the furrows just left here by the stumpy little legs of the hippo charging out of the water? Or does it have to do with the droppings?

David began the day with a course on "spoor", in actual fact, he explains, anything that permits the tracking of the animal. It can be the dung, paw-or hoof-prints, twigs or branches broken in passing, spider-webs snatched from the brush. It can even be the measure of the animal's pace: drawing an isosceles triangle can reveal the height at the shoulder of an impala, as well as the extent of its leap, known to have reached fourteen meters.

Sidelight to the matter of a "spoor": the scrub hare lives below ground and its young are born completely helpless. It therefore defecates a soft pellet that can be re-eaten, in order to leave no trace. This form of ruminant belongs to the species with a *caecum* digestion. In general terms, however, the balance of nature depends on manure. If nature's greatest miracle is defined in the recycling of its resources, dung is the key. The hippo even enriches the water with its droppings. The elephant, as a matter of fact, digests only forty percent of its dietary intake, so a number of other species, including the termite, enter the "food chain" by means of its excrement. After we returned from Africa Tomás regaled friends with his "doctorate", as he described it, in matters of dung, and people would demand that each of us tell our personal version of the journey. Tomás had learned to identify the droppings of every animal on every game drive, while I was taking pictures and making notes, plumping up my "literary sketchbook".

"So what we have here," Tomás proclaims, "is poetry and field notes, as opposed to manure".

The phenomenon of the "food chain" is illustrated by means of the famous "sequence of the dead buffalo": 1) The lion that has killed the buffalo tears open the skin and enjoys its share so that, 2) vultures can pick up the scraps while, 3) hyenas or jackals divide the leavings until 4) bone chips are salvaged by the eagles, hawks and, especially, the vultures again. 5) Tortoises and vultures will eat the hyena dung, then 6) the "hide" or "museum" beetle will eat the drying skin while 7) the "larva" or "horn" moth lays eggs inside the horns which serve as their sustenance. 8) Anything left the termites will take until the 9) final trophy of the skull, bleached to crumble in the sun, is returned to the soil in the form of bone meal.

The termites, of course, are the great masters of ecological recycling. Their sheer numbers, and their impact on the landscape, dominate every aspect of life in Africa. If the elephant consumes only ten percent of a tree or bush, the termites account for the rest. In fact, the termites act on most of the continent's discarded vegetation in order to accelerate the process of decomposition, and thus facilitate the alimentary diversity for all the species.

A million termites amount to only a small family. They are blind, yet create among the world's most graceful architecture, "castles of clay" that weigh tens of tons and reach five or six meters in height, proportionately equivalent to a man-made structure four kilometers tall. They build their astonishing monument-mounds in a variety of styles, depending on the climate, using their saliva as cement, and design them to avoid the ultra-violet rays of the sun, to which the pale creatures are inordinately sensitive — they are, in fact, so pale and so transparent that their food during its digestive process is perfectly visible, like a cutaway diagram in a scientific display — and to permit their being able to carry out their relentless labors, of construction, procreation or defense, during the daylight hours.

Termites have been on the earth for over one hundred million years. Their nearest relative is the cockroach. They are entirely herbivorous, as opposed to their enemies the ants, particularly the black army ants, notorious predators. Their exquisitely intricate tunnels can extend for thirty meters and the labyrinths follow an elaborate pattern, confected of sticks, stumps or elephant dung under an outer casing or awning of dirt and clay.

These are built during the dry months, before the rainy season can wash them away. As the food inside is consumed, the levels of the materials are altered, so are gradually replaced by the earth, converted by the rains into pliable mud, until only the hardened mound remains, whose apertures and shafts—without affecting the life of the termites inside—additionally serve as nests or refuge, temporary or permanent, for other animals. The chimneys, which release warm air and keep the termites cool at their labors within the depths of their "underground city", and the fungus gardens of their food supply, at this latitude always face east/west, leaning toward the east, to regulate the temperature or to compensate for the prevailing winds.

According to naturalist-photographers' Joan and Alan Root's remarkable film, probably one of the most prodigious nature documentaries ever produced (**BBC, Anglia Survival**, 1982), the vast and amorphous queen dominates the colony. She is a fertility machine, capable of producing literally millions of eggs each day, but more than that: she produces as well a chemical code that instructs her hierarchy of soldiers and workers as to the affairs of their community: when to build new walls, when to engender more soldiers or fewer workers (or the reverse), how much vegetable matter to obtain or discard, when to take the fungi outdoors into the daylight to produce another generation of mushrooms. The strict hierarchy that involves all of her population therefore follows her instructions, replies with additional information and ultimately cares for her, since she is helpless. Only two percent of her subjects are soldiers, in two sizes, all female. They are sterile. Workers are of both genders but are also sterile. Since the queen is too gigantic to move, she remains locked in a dark chamber for life, accompanied by her king. He is only a fraction of her size and needs a full fifteen minutes to walk the equivalent of her length.

When her productivity fades she is "licked to death". By that time, during a fleeting fifteen minutes on one night, and one night only, during the rainy season, another sector of the termite population, called "ailites" or "winged ones", emerge on frail white wings that they later discard, in order to continue and renew the cycle, leaving the mound to the casual vagaries of any subsequent tenant, or to the weather, until it erodes and collapses. All it takes is a single pair of termites to begin the cycle all over again.

∭

After a leisurely lunch, making time to see which way the weather might blow, we are surprised, for the wind has died down. The afternoon seems very quiet. Meg and Cora have gone off to Kariba to run errands. The two South African sisters caught up with us, but then decided to go off on a game drive with David.

John, our Australian friend, is equally at loose ends. We make up a committee and go off in search of Richard who, more than anything else to get rid of us, suggests we take a boat across the lake to visit "The Place of the Buffalo", Sanyati Gorge. A nice old farmer from South Africa, engrossed in some sort of dialogue with Richard, seconds the motion, by telling us how lovely it is, how remarkable the vegetation, how serene the river that now empties into Lake Kariba, how extraordinary the fauna, the rock formations, the sense of complete isolation. Together they have us convinced.

Richard sends us off in one of the flat-bottomed speedboats with a guide named Arthur, one of the boys who had initially taken our bags off the truck when we arrived here, and a pilot named Gabriel. The lake, however, is choppier than we had thought. Since I sat in the rear of the boat on the left-hand side I caught all the spray. As long as my handbag, plastic-lined but not impermeable, with my camera, film and notebook, remained dry, nothing else seemed to matter, and it felt rather refreshing, though I was getting soaked on just one side, and Tomás, sitting on the right-hand side of the boat, looked over and realized what was happening, so suggested I change places with John, who was wearing shorts. Among other considerations, I was still wearing bandages and they were getting wet. Though I had nearly recovered, Tomas continued to dress the burns twice a day and I kept them under bandages, more than anything else to protect them from the sun. "Who knows what germs there may be in the water," Tomás insisted. "I see no point in taking chances."

19.

CAROL IN SANYATI GORGE

It took much longer to cross the lake than we had originally calculated. The boat struggled and lurched against the waves, its flat bottom just skimming, with no depth of a keel for it to stabilize. We even considered turning back but the entrance to the gorge was so close now, its surface like glass beckoning to us. It seemed foolish to waste all that time and effort.

During the dry season the rocky, steep walls of the canyon are known for their baboon colonies, and the many scorpions that are their trophy, but when the rains begin the canyon comes alive with "klipspringer", another local species of antelope, with bushbuck, Vervet monkeys, felines of all sorts, buffalo and, Arthur tells us, the occasional elephant, though this is hard to believe in such hostile— steep and rocky— terrain.

The tan and blue reflection of the canyon walls in the river also mirrors the fish eagle, clinging to its fragile nest on the top of a tree that had been taken over when the water rose and which now swings precariously over the rocks. The sodium residue has marked a water line, and this has risen and fallen a number of times, leaving behind a web of tangled roots clinging desperately to the boulders.

We ease into a tributary, an intersection of the main channel with a steep canyon on either side, forming a cross, all the time overseen by the cackling sentry of the Chacma baboon. His family follows him in single file. They tip pebbles down the slopes at our passing, but are more bemused than aggressive. These baboons are joined by others. They traipse in glee along the edge of a cliff in search of scorpions or fruit. If one of the youngsters chances on a tidbit the elders, the "Gentlemen of the Bush" as Arthur calls them, "because they walk like public officials", slap him across the face and take it from him.

A giant kingfisher grabs onto the branch of a dry, dead tree, while Vervet monkeys adhere to the "sandpaper" tree, and the *baobabs* on the canyon rim. Yellow mimosa blooms reflect in the tan and brown edges of the blue water and a crocodile slips furtively off a rock, sliding into the water with only the faintest telltale splash. A fork-tailed *drongo* nips and badgers a hawk-eagle, driving it from its nest. The steady, panting heat has nearly dried my clothes and I feel almost euphoric, though the canyon was hardly worth the effort of the trip.

Where the gorge narrows and the river virtually disappears, the way is nearly blocked by the "Floating Stones" (for the tremendous size of the enormous flat boulders). Here the canyon dissolves into a steep track, but instead of ending it climbs farther up into the tumbled rocks. Perhaps when the rains come it will become a waterfall.

Gabriel, taking the sun in the rear by the engine, drops a pop bottle on a string into the water until it fills, then drains it dry. The heat, even so late in the day, is fierce, and soon we are all filling our pop bottles with the river water, which is fresh and sweet.

The shadows are growing long and we have a great distance yet to cover. Surely the lake will be calmer now that the sun has dropped. We turn back along the main gorge, passing two other boats on the way. A man in a vest, obviously dedicated to sport fishing, holds up a still-flapping "tiger fish" and we applaud.

20.

SANYATI TIGER FISH

With this we are distracted for a moment. When we look again we have left the quiet waters and the darkening canyon walls of the gorge, and have shot, as if we had hit the bottom of a slope on a toboggan, into the lake's full fury. Nyami-Nyami is being especially vindictive. The wind is so shrill we are unable to call from the bow to the rear where Gabriel is struggling with the engine. The waves engulf us in seconds.

I started to laugh. This was nature gone mad. My eye caught sight of the life jackets tucked into a compartment under the bow and after passing them around to the others I grabbed one for myself, but I used it to shield my chest and lap, in which I made a nest for my handbag. "If my camera and notebook get wet," I thought to myself gaily, "I am doomed."

Meantime, the boat was swamped. "Damn," I mutter under my breath, "I had just managed to dry out." The fact is, we were all doomed. We might very well have *really* been doomed, and considered ourselves fortunate, to disappear mercifully under the waves, without having to battle crocodiles or tiger fish. There was no hope of making it back to Fothergill. Our best chance, signaled Gabriel, was to put in at the cove of the Sanyati Lodge, which he indicated with a wave of his trembling black hand. The cabins loomed high above us, on the ridge that formed one wall of the Gorge. But where was the cove? I saw nothing but cliffs.

The flat bottom of the speedboat was skidding from side to side, the engine completely out of the water. The waves tossed us like toothpicks from crest to crest. What was it Eliud, our driver in Tanzania, had said about going faster when the road was rough? He thought this would send him flying from bump to bump. I was still laughing, a bit hysterically, and the others had caught my laughter, like a contagious disease.

The full realization of our predicament had yet to set in, and we lost all track of time. This was to have been an afternoon's excursion, after all, a "fun" side trip into a little known corner of an enigmatic countryside.

Suddenly, miraculously, the waters stopped lashing. The waves, that had blinded us, had subsided. The rocking of the unhappy little boat had ceased, though its planks continued to groan. Long, dark arms reached out to help us ashore. There was no dock or wharf, just shallow water and pebbles. A man with thinning blond hair going gray, stocky, very self-assured, was sizing up the situation, talking to Gabriel and looking at us intently.

"I had just gotten dry in the gorge," I heard myself say, inanely, while the water sputtered down my Outback hat into my face. The man, instead of answering, indicated a footpath out of the cove, that zigzagged up a sharp incline. We had to struggle up one cliff, then down the other side into a larger cove that was strewn with debris, with boats bobbing on the stony shore, then up another hill beyond.

At the top of the path a lane, between stunted and shriveled bushes, edged along a line of small wooden cottages. These ascended a steep embankment until they reached a level place at the top of the ridge, that framed the entrance to Sanyati Gorge.

We finally reached the last cottage, really a thatched hut open on all sides, that gave onto a view over the enraged water of the enormous lake, an inland sea, and eternal. It seemed we were hang-gliding, with the lake spread out like a carpet below.

Arthur, John and Tomás, all talking at once, tried to explain what had happened. Gabriel had stayed behind at the cove with the boat. Our host, Hans, a businessman from Harare who had always wanted to "get away from it all", had built a small, rustic lodge as isolated as it could possibly be, with no roads, no airstrip, no dock. The place could only be reached by small boat. There was a radio, however, and while he questioned us, he was getting Fothergill on one of his frequencies. "Richard?" he queried. "You have a problem!"

Meanwhile, Hans' companion, Beverly, whisked me to one of the cottages for a shower. "Wonderful," I gushed. "A hot shower cures nearly everything."

"No hot water," replied Beverly, cryptically, but she smiled. At least we could scrub down, dry off with a rough towel, and dress in the souvenir t-shirts with the legend "Sanyati", and a comic design of a crocodile and, in the absence of any other available garments, an extra towel as a *pareu.*

Hans, Tomás and John, who had simply toweled off, were hanging their clothes on a branch. John, the wry and sophisticated Australian, was making urbane chit chat with Hans. We were settling in very happily for what promised to be a delightful evening, and I was on the verge of asking for a brandy, when Hans stood up abruptly and looked at us very seriously. "This is the situation," he began.

No one spoke. We were suddenly very subdued. "It will take Richard at least two hours to drive around to this part of the lake to pick you up at the rangers' camp."

"Why can't we spend the night and go back tomorrow?" I asked. I was already visualizing the view of the lake in the dawn light.

"Because there's no room," replied Hans. "The hotel is full."

"But I see no one about," I insisted.

"They're out fishing, or hiking, but will be back soon. So what you will do is the following: my boys will take you back to the large cove and you can borrow my pontoon. It will get you up the lake past the mouth of Sanyati Gorge to the rangers' landing, but you must go right away. It's nearly dark and there are no lights. I can loan you a couple of kerosene lanterns but that's all there is. And remember, the lakeshore is full of stumps and dead trees. Not to mention crocodiles. There are no charts. The rangers will meet you. I've already contacted them by radio. Richard is on his way there now. Gabriel will stay with the pontoon and bring it back in the morning, and at the same time pick up the speedboat. You will take Arthur back with you. You owe me thirty-six Zimbabwe dollars for the t-shirts. The drinks are my pleasure. Good luck to you. Now, let's get going."

We were too surprised to argue, so we rolled up our wet things, scrambled as best we could down the dark hillside and stalked single file back across the larger of the two coves. Hans made a sad, sweeping gesture at the sight of the debris strewn everywhere. "My shipment of thatch had just come in for the new cottages. We were trying to unload when we saw you flounder." We shook hands and said goodbye.

We had to splash out barefoot to board the pontoon. We then headed again into the nightmare thrashing of the enraged lake, no less mollified with the coming of night. The pontoon was of course more steady than the flat-bottomed speedboat but Gabriel, if he could have done, would happily have gone livid with fear. He was absolutely terrified. So were the rest of us, but as John said, there was no point making an issue of it.

Trust in fate, I thought to myself. I had promised my son I would be very careful on this trip, and not do anything foolish. Here I was, with burned legs, dripping bandages, and a shipwreck in Zimbabwe.

Meantime, Tomás and John were too busy as pilots to think of anything else. They would have done well on the Mississippi, in Mark

Twain's day. With the lanterns poised high in the air and Arthur on his stomach at the edge of the pontoon, peering and squinting into the water, we chugged along slowly, very slowly, through the raging waves, while the clouds lowered over a daylight hopelessly spent.

It seemed an eternity but we finally saw the shadows of the dead trees in the water and a glint of white paint on the rangers' dock. It took more time, of careful maneuvering, to bring in the pontoon, but the waves were less angry in this quiet bay, the stars were coming out, and the rangers were lined up, their rifles slung over their shoulders, their arms outstretched, to pull us onto their dock. There were no perceptible crocodiles.

I said goodbye to Gabriel, to thank him for a difficult job, very well done. His hand was like ice. I told him to come up with us by the fire but he just shook his head, indicating the pontoon with a vague wave, his eyes rolling back in his head. So we made a human chain and link by link, with trembling knees, climbed up the steep path through the woods. A number of the rangers went off to their cots in the tent pitched to one side of a clearing. The others, the more sociable ones, remained with us around the campfire, heating coffee on their grill.

But for the flames there was no light at all. The black faces in the black night, except for the glow of their eyes and the sheen of their white teeth, were invisible. It was only with the camera's flash that I was able to see where we were or find the chair they offered, to sit down to wait for Richard to arrive.

Then the moon came out: the shameless, outrageous full moon, an augur moon, an omen moon, the moon that lighted Richard's way to the rangers' camp and that helped us climb inside the big, open truck.

Richard, of course, was less than joyful. After a muttered greeting he never spoke, had brought no blankets; and even forgot to put the truck in gear, so that it started sliding down the hill as we tried to scramble inside, when the hand brake gave way.

We cleared the boulders, waving goodbye and goodnight to the jovial rangers, then started along the road that skirted the lake, another two hours to Fothergill. The landscape, bathed in full moonlight, seemed more rapturous than ghostly. Our headlights caught the hare watching us from under a bush, a solitary elephant just to one side of the road, a band of startled duiker. The "night jars", like the fluttering ravens in a story by Poe or the Rocky Horror Show, swept over the open truck like a bomber escort. Low branches snatched at our damp hair, to the lullaby of the lumpy murmur of the frogs by the lake's edge. A cloud passed over the moon then cleared again. When it emerged, it seemed brighter than ever. Shameless, indeed.

As we rounded the bend into Fothergill, where the herds were settling down for the night, to the right and left of us we saw dozens of pairs of small red lights. They were the eyes of the impala in the moonlight, caught by the headlights on the truck, leaping—seemingly in slow motion—out of our way, hurtling through the dark then turning to stare, their eyes flaring crimson.

I can see them still, in the moonlight through my bedroom window, when sleep fails or when the woods where I walk in the morning are shrouded in mist. I see the pairs of eyes, the tawny leaping bodies; and especially that night at Fothergill, driving home from our shipwreck, with the elephants silhouetted against the lake and the hippos thundering busily across the road on the scampering legs that seem to leave no trace but which in fact dig deep furrows in the red clay: those eyes that burn, like a brand on the memory.

$$\int\!\int\!\int$$

Meg and Cora were waiting up for us. The electricity was still on, and the bar was open. They had personally prepared our dinner and had tender steaks ready to put on the carefully primed fire. The two sisters from South Africa, lurking in the shadows, were waiting discreetly for a detailed account of our adventure. Meg's lighthearted warmth and pretended nonchalance betrayed her concern. Richard was very sullen. He had evidently been dressed down for letting us go.

Silently, with bowed heads, we saw Asma and Janice in the shadows. They were praying.

WEDNESDAY, NOVEMBER 15

The lake was still surging the following morning. The pale blue sky was a bit more sullen in the East around the still rising sun. Yet the dancing birds were out, and darting insects. Two worlds seemed to be standing off, the stormy one and the fresh and frolicking one, where the weaver birds call to their mates and the females respond with approval of the nests. The fierce heat of the day began to rise, sending off the chill breeze of the dawn, as we had tea with John before he departed back to Perth. We stayed in contact for many months, but then he remarried and no longer replied to our letters.

After one last game drive, this time with Meg herself, a new boatman took us sadly back across a quieter but still restless lake. He said they would all miss us at Fothergill, we had livened up the place. We had challenged Nyami-Nyami the River God; or perhaps it was because of him that we were rescued.

We must wait at the dreary landing for about an hour until the bus charges down the dust track to pick us up, to take us to the airport. There are the two of us, as well as Asma and Janice, and two Swiss girls working for a development program in Zaïre, along with a young couple from Adelaide. We leave them sitting on the logs while we take a walk to look out over the enormous lake, its convoluted edges, the paths that cross and re-cross and criss-cross the hard red earth and barely greening trees. The surface of the water is now beveled glass, reflecting a cloudless sky.

THURSDAY, NOVEMBER 16

A quiet day in Harare, reassembling the luggage, shopping for hair straightener for a friend in Mexico, and visiting with Asma and Janice, who have joined us for tea at the famous Maeckles Hotel downtown. For a long time we corresponded, until they were ejected from Saudi Arabia and somehow we lost touch.

FRIDAY, NOVEMBER 17

After an early breakfast, the flight to Nairobi. We are met by people from the Mexican Embassy. We stop on Muindi Mbingu Street to pick up more hematite beads at Aquarius, then drive through Nairobi's privileged residential suburb for an excellent dinner at the Residence. A dancing drizzle freshens the lawn and a shocking green chameleon appears on the branches of a bush under the dining room window. We had originally planned to dine on mangrove crab and Kenya lobster at Tamarind, but the Ambassador had been called to Geneve on a diplomatic emergency and his wife was receiving her daughter's friends for a birthday party at home. Another Scorpio. She blows out the candles on her cake with a jubilant *Si kukuni yako.*

A&K returns us to the airport to board our night flight back to Paris, on the plane that has just arrived from Bujumbura, the capital of Burundi, and Kigali, capital of Rwanda. The Tonga walking stick with the carving of Nyami-Nyami the River God is still intact, though it was misplaced a couple of times. We try to keep a close watch on it. A deity's protection is not to be taken lightly.

"A pilgrim's reward is the memory of having been there."

AFTERWORD

It took a long time to return from Africa. I would still wear boots and a pith helmet to friends' luncheons in Cuernavaca, my Masai jewelry, the stunning pectoral that Tomás created from African amber and Ethiopian crosses—a masterpiece. I was obsessed. And to my friends, a little ridiculous. Then I sculpted African animals and cast them in bronze. I pasted up photos in albums, typed up my notes, prepared the first draft of this book, and then filed it away. It had to percolate.

Only two or three years later I found a lost dog and adopted her, and together we struck out on foot through the Pedregal where I live, where the only wildlife is rather tame—though one neighbor has a lion and another an aviary—and then we expanded our expeditions into nearby parks where there might be a deer, a bobcat, an owl; and finally into the mountains, following the trails across the extinct volcano cones and pine woods, the prints of bush rabbit and rattlesnake. We were intrepid explorers opening the trackless lands of the inner mind and deeper soul.

I ended with a collection of lost or abandoned dogs and my explorations lasted some ten years, my reading and research continued, until one day I realized I had put the last dog to sleep and my walks no longer had any meaning. Tomás, who was never fond of my dogs or enthused by the hikes in the mountains, begged me to stop. "I'll buy you a stuffed animal of your choice, but this has to end. Dog hair in the living room, the urine deodorants, rising before dawn to walk the dogs." I was still following the shameless full moon, but I was in Mexico now, not Africa.

There were other trips, different moonlight, many albums of photos, and notebooks transcribed. I learned to use a computer, and the older manuscripts had to be uploaded and revised. There were other exhibits of my sculpture, with other motifs. Africa began to fade, until one day, cleaning out files and straightening up the library, we found the Africa manuscripts that Tomás had long ago taken to the copyright office but which had never been uploaded, one in English and the other its translation to Spanish. "This is wonderful," he said. "It's time to do something about it." Here it is.

ABOUT THE AUTHOR: CAROL MILLER FROM MEXICO!

Carol Miller from Mexico! So called the footman at the Israeli Embassy in London. It was a formal dinner in 1962. Carol Miller from Mexico, the only Carol Miller in Mexico, had already covered all of Latin America as a journalist and correspondent, was touring Europe and would reach the Middle East, under contract from then Director of Tourism, Teddy Kolleck, to report on historical events. In the intervening years she has covered the world, circled it many times, and captured in her books and sculptures the essence of art, history and personal anecdote. Then why was Africa so special? What aroused the longing for her lost childhood? And what had honed such a keen eye for her shrewd observations? "No use arguing with pure magic," she says.

BIBLIOGRAPHY

Adamson, Joy: **Born Free,** London, Collins-Fontana Books, 1966.

Adamson, Joy: **Forever Free,** New York, Bantom, 1967.

Adamson, Joy: **Living Free,** London, Collins-Fontana Books, 1967.

Amin, Mohamed, Duncan Willetts y Alastair Matheson: **Railway Across the Equator,** London, The Bodley Head, 1986.

Ammann, Karl y Kathrine: **The Hunter and the Hunted,** London, The Bodley Head, 1989.

Ardrey, Robert: **African Genesis,** London, Collins-Fontana, 6ª reimpresión, 1970.

Ardrey, Robert: **The Social Contract,** New York, Atheneum, 1970.

Ardrey, Robert: **The Territorial Imperative,** New York, Delta, 1966.

Bachelard, Gastón: **Psicoanálisis del Fuego,** Madrid, Alianza Editorial, 1966.

Baker, Carlos: **Ernest Hemingway: A Life Story,** New York, Charles Scribner's Sons, 1969.

Barber, Benjamin & Patrick Watson: **The Struggle For Democracy,** Boston, Little, Brown & Co., 1988.

Barton, J.G.: **Flores Silvestres,** México, Queromón Editores, S.A., 1964.

Beckwith, Carol and Angela Fisher: New York, Harry N. Abrams, Inc., 1990.

Bentsen, Cheryl: **Maasai Days,** New York, Summit Books, 1989.

Bernal, Martin: **Black Athena: The Afroasiatic Roots of Classical Civilization,** New Jersey USA, Rutgers University Press, quinta re-impresión, 1990.

Blundell, M.: **Wild Flowers of East Africa,** London, Collins, 1987.

Bridges, William: **The Bronx Zoo Book of Wild Animals,** New York, The New York Zoological Society y Golden Press, 1968.

Broadhurst, P.S.: **The Science of Animal Behavior,** London, Pelican, 1966.

Bronowski, J.: **The Ascent of Man,** Boston, Little, Brown & Co., 1973.

Bueno, Miguel: **Introducción a la antropología formal,** México, Fondo de Cultural Económica, 1963.

Butcher, Tim: **Blood River, A Journey to Africa's Broken Heart,** New York, Grove Press, 2008.

Canaway, W.H.: **The Hunter and the Horns,** London, Penguin, 1968.

Caputo, Robert: **Journey Up the Nile,** Charlottesville, Virginia (USA), Thomason-Grant, Inc., 1988.

Chamber's **Mineralogical Dictionary**, New York, Chemical Publishing Co., Inc., 1948.

Cinotti, Mia: **Arte del Mundo Antiguo,** México-Buenos Aires, Editorial Hermés, 1964.

Cole, J.P.: **Geography of World Affairs,** London, Pelican, 1966.

Condé, Maryse: **The Children of Segu,** New York, Viking, 1989.

Conrad, Josef, Morton Dauwen Zabel, Ed.: **The Portable Conrad,** New York, The Viking Press, 1947.

Cotterell, Arthur: **A Dictionary of World Mythology,** New York, Perigee Books, 1979.

Cowley, Malcolm: **A Second Flowering: Works and Days of the Lost Generation,** New York, The Viking Press, segunda edición 1973, esp. *Hemingway, The Old Lion, p. 216.*

Crim, Keith (Editor General): **The Perennial Dictionary of World Religions,** San Francisco (USA), Harper & Row, 1981.

Dalton, Stephen: **Borne on the Wind,** New York, Reader's Digest Press, 1975.

Dance, S. Peter, Ed.: **The Encyclopedia of Shells,** Dorset, UK, Blandford Press, 1977.

Dart, Raymond A. y Dennis Craig: **Aventuras con el Eslabón Perdido,** México, Fondo de Cultura Económica, 1962.

Darwin, Charles: **The Origin of Species,** London, J.M. Dent & Sons, 1967.

Darwin, Charles: **The Voyage of the Beagle,** London, J.M. Dent & Sons, 1961.

Dinesen, Isak (Karen Blixen): **Anecdotes of Destiny,** Londres, Penguin Books, re-edición 1988.

Dinesen, Isak: **Isak Dinesen's Africa,** London, Bantam Press (Transworld Publishers), 1985.

Dinesen, Isak: **Seven Gothic Tales,** London, Penguin, 1952.

Dinesen, Isak (Karen Blixen): **Out of Africa,** London, Penguin, 1988.

Diop, Cheikh Anta (Mercer Cook, translated from the French): **The African Origin of Civilization: Myth or Reality,** USA, Lawrence Hill & Co., 1974.

Dugard, Martin: **Into Africa, The Epic Adventures of Stanley & Livingstone,** New York, Broadway Books, 2004.

Durrell, Gerald: **A Zoo in my Luggage,** London, Penguin, 1966

Durrell, Gerald: **Encounters With Animals,** London, Penguin Books, 1967.

Durrell, Gerald: **The Overloaded Ark,** London, Penguin, 1962.

Elisofon, Eliot: **The Nile,** Introduction by Laurens van der Post, New York, Viking Press, 1964.

Ezra, Kate: **Royal Art of Benin,** New York, The Metropolitan Museum of Art, 1992.

Fisher, Angela: **Africa Adorned,** New York, Harry N. Abrams, 1984.

Forés, Oriol Galí: **El Turbulento Siglo XX,** España, Editorial Marín, S.A., 1970, two volumes.

Fromm, Erich: **The Anatomy of Human Destructiveness,** New York, Holt, Rinehart & Winston, 1973.

Gordon, René: **Africa, A Continent Revealed,** New York, St. Martín's Press, 1981.

Graves, Robert, introducción: **New Larousse Encyclopedia of Mythology,** London, Paul Hamlyn, 1969.

Grzimek, Bernhard y Michael: **Serengeti Shall Not Die,** London, Collins-Fontana, 1967.

Hanby, J. y D. Bygott: **Lion's Share,** Nueva York, Collins & Houghton Mifflin Co., 1981.

Hanby, Jeannette y David Bygott: **Ngorongoro Conservation Area,** Dar es Salaam, Tanzania, Wildlife Conservation Society of Tanzania, 1986.

Hastings, Michael: **Sir Richard Francis Burton,** New York, Coward, McCann & Geoghegan, Inc., 1978.

Hemingway, Ernest: **The Essential Hemingway,** London, Penguin Books, 1969, esp. *The Short Happy Life of Francis Macomber, p. 413 y The Snows of Kilimanjaro, p. 443.*

Hemingway, Ernest: **The Green Hills of Africa,** New York, Collier Books (MacMillan Publishing Co.), 1987.

Huxley, Elspeth: **Out in the Midday Sun,** London, Penguin, 1985.

Huxley, Elspeth: **The Flame Trees of Thika,** London, Penguin Books, 1962.

Johanson C. Donald and Maitland Edey: **Lucy, The Beginnings of Humankind, How Our Oldest Human Ancestor Was Discovered—and Who She Was,** New York etc., Simon & Schuster, 1981.

Johanson C., Donald and Kate Wong: **Lucy's Legacy, The Quest For Human Origins,** New York, Three Rivers Press, 2009.

Kaj, Arhem: **Pastoral Man in the Garden of Eden,** Uppsala, Suecia, Uppsala Research Reports in Anthropology, 1985.

Köhler, Wolfgang, **The Mentality of Apes,** London, Pelican, 1957.

Künkel, Reinhard: **Elephants,** New York, Harry N. Abrams, 1989.

Lawick-Goodall, Jane: **In the Shadow of Man,** Boston, Houghton Mifflin Co., 1971.

Liebowitz, Daniel M.D. and Charles Pearson: **The Last Expedition, Stanley's Mad Journey Through the Congo,** New York and London, W.W. Norton & Company, 2005.

Lorenz, Konrad: **King Soloman's Ring,** New York, Time, Inc. Books Division, 1962.

Lorenz, Konrad: **On Aggression,** London, Metheun & Co., Ltd., 1969.

Lovell, Mary S.: **A Rage to Live, A Biography of Richard and Isabel Burton,** New York and London, W.W. Norton & Company, 1998.

Lovell, Mary S.: The Churchills in Love and War, New York, W.W. Norton & Co., 2011

Malraux, André: **La Condición Humana,** Barcelona, Edhasa, 1971.

Man and Animal (Man Through His Art), London, Educational Productions, Ltd., 1965.

Markham, Beryl: **The Splendid Outcast,** New York, Dell Publishing, 1987.

Markham, Beryl: **West With the Night,** London, Virago Press, 1984.

Matthiessen, Peter (text), Eliot Porter (photos): **The Tree Where Man Was Born and The African Experience,** New York, E.P. Dutton & Co., 1972.

May, Inés: **Simple Swahili,** Nairobi, 1980.

Menzel-Tettenborn, Helga and Günter Radtke: **Animals in Their World,** New York, Grosset & Dunlap, 1973.

Milne, Lorus and Margery: **The Nature of Life,** New York, Crown Publishers, 1970.

Moorehead, Alan: **No Room in the Ark,** London, Penguin, 1964.

Moorehead, Alan, **The Blue Nile,** London, Hamish Hamilton, segunda edición, 1962.

Moorehead, Alan: **The White Nile,** New York, Harper & Row, revision 1971.

Morris, Desmond: **La Biología del Arte,** México, Siglo Veintiuno Editores, 1971.

Morris, Desmond: **El Mono Desnudo,** Barcelona, Plaza & Janés, S.A., 1969.

Moucha, J.: **Las mariposas nocturnas,** México, Queromón Editores, S.A., 1966.

National Wildlife Federation, **Kingdom of Cats,** Washington, D.C. (USA), 1987.

Pischel, Gina: **A World History of Art,** New York, Golden Press, 1968, esp. *The Impact of African Art, pp. 648-9.*

Pitman, Dick: **Zimbabwe Portrait,** Harare, Zimbabwe, Clive Murphy of Modus Publications (pvt), Ltd., Second Edition, no date.

Ricciardi, Mirella: **Vanishing Africa,** London, William Collins Son & Co., Ltd., 1974.

Ritts, Herb: **Africa,** Boston, New York, Toronto, London, A Bulfinch Press Book/Little, Brown and Company, 1994.

Rodríguez de la Fuente: Félix: **Fauna,** México, Salvat Editores, 1970.

Salim, Ahmed I.: **People of the Coast (Kenya's People),** Nairobi, Evans Brothers (Kenya) Limited, 1985.

Schaller, George: **The Year of the Gorilla,** London, Penguin, reimpresión 1967.

Schildkrout, Enid and Curtis A. Keim: **African Reflections, Art From Northeastern Zaire,** New York, American Museum of Natural History, 1990.

Scott, Jonathan: **The Great Migration,** London, Elm Tree Books, 1988.

Shah, Idries, introducción Robert Graves: **The Sufis,** London, Jonathan Cape, 1964.

Simon, Hilda: **The Splendor of Iridescence,** New York, Dodd, Mead & Co., 1971.

Smart, Ninian: **The Long Search,** Boston, Little, Brown & Co., 1977.

Smith, David Lovatt: **Amboseli, Nothing Short of a Miracle,** Nairobi, East African Publishing House, 1986.

Snelson, Deborah, Ed.: **Lake Manyara National Park,** Tanzania National Parks and the African Wildlife Foundation, Revised 1986.

Snelson, Deborah, Ed.: **Serengeti National Park,** Tanzania National Parks and The African Wildlife Foundation, Revised 1986.

Taylor, Kim: **Discovery Guide to West Africa (The Niger and Gambia River Route),** London, Michael Haag, 1989.

Thompson, Ralph: **An Artist's Safari,** New York, E.P. Dutton & Co., Inc., 1970.

Tichy, Herbert: **Kenya,** Innsbruck, Austria, Pinguin-Verlag, 1980.

Van der Post, Laurens: **The Heart of the Hunter,** London, Penguin, 1968.

Van der Post, Laurens: **The Lost World of the Kalahari,** London, Penguin, 1968.

Van der Post, Laurens: **Venture to the Interior,** London, Penguin, 1964.

Van Over, Raymond: **Sun Songs: Creation Myths From Around the World,** New York, Mentor-New American Library, 1980.

Verghese, Dr. Abraham: **My Own Country, a Doctor's Story** (New York, Simon & Schuster, 1994, p. 251)

Wardwell, Allen (text), Bobby Hansson (photos): **African Sculpture,** Philadelphia (USA), Philadelphia Museum of Art, 1986-87.

Williams, John Alden, Ed.: **Islam,** New York, George Braziller, 1962.

Williams, J.H.: **The Spotted Deer,** London, Penguin, 1961.

Williams, Lt. Col. J.H.: **Elephant Bill,** London, Penguin Books, 1966.

Wilson, Alison: **Guidebook to the Masai Mara Reserve,** Nairobi, Design Horizons International, 1983.

Winkler, Josef. R.: **El libro de los coleópteros,** México, Queromón Editores, S.A., 1965.

∫∫∫

Made in the USA
San Bernardino, CA
12 April 2014